THE ASSOCIATION OF EDUCATIONAL PUBLISHERS

Lamp of Learning Series

PUBLISHING WITHOUT BOUNDARIES

MICHAEL N. ROSS

How to Think, Work, and Win in the Global Marketplace

A Lamp of Learning Series Publication

Published by The Association of Educational Publishers
510 Heron Drive, Suite 201, Logan Township, NJ 08085 U.S.A.
www.edpress.org

ISBN-13: 978-0-9789857-0-7
ISBN-10: 0-9789857-0-2

Printed in the United States of America.

This publication is designed to provide accurate and authoritative information with regard to the subject matter covered. It is sold with the understanding that the publisher is not engaged in rendering legal, accounting, or other professional advice. If legal advice or other expert assistance is required, the services of a competent professional person should be sought.

— From a *Declaration of Principles* jointly adopted by a Committee of the American Bar Association and a Committee of Publishers and Associations

TRADEMARKS

Throughout this book trademarked names are used. Rather than put a trademark symbol in every occurrence of a trademarked name, we state we are using the names only in an editorial fashion and to the benefit of the trademark owner with no intention of infringement of the trademark. All trademarks or service marks are the property of their respective owners.

Cover design by Andrea Burke.

Contents

About Michael N. Ross

 Michael Ross is the Senior Vice President and Education General Manager at Encyclopaedia Britannica, Inc., where he heads worldwide electronic and print publishing. Prior to joining Britannica in 2002, he was the Executive Vice President and Publisher of World Book, Inc., and has held executive positions at other publishing companies, including NTC Publishing Group. He began his publishing career as an editor for Time-Life Books and worked for three years in their Tokyo bureau.

His products and publications have won the highest industry awards, including the Distinguished Achievement and the Golden Lamp Awards from the Association of Educational Publishers; the GLI Award, presented at the Bologna Children's Book Fair; *Learning* Magazine's Teacher's Choice Award; *PC Magazine*'s Editor's Choice Award; Parent's Choice Award; *Family PC*'s Top 100 Award; and the Software & Information Industry Association's Codie Award.

Michael served on the executive committee and the board of directors of the Association of Educational Publishers, including a term as president from 2002 to 2003. He also serves on the board of Intellisophic, the world's largest provider of taxonomic content. He is listed in *Who's Who in America* and in October 2002 was inducted into *Printmedia*'s Production Executives' Hall of Fame.

He has contributed to several industry publications, including the *Experts' Guide to the K-12 School Market*. His first book, *Publishing without Borders*, was published in 2003. He has a B.A., *summa cum laude*, from the University of Minnesota, an M.A. from Brandeis University, and a certificate from Stanford University's Advanced Management College. Michael would be delighted to receive comments and feedback on this book or discuss your particular publishing interests. Please contact him at: michaelnross@comcast.net.

Introduction

Every literate society and culture has its own publishing industry serving its internal needs. Because publishing tends to be a language- and culture-specific industry that requires intimate connection with its market, it's extremely difficult for a publisher from one culture to establish a meaningful presence in another. Even when multinational conglomerates acquire local publishing companies, domestic publishing remains fiercely independent. It has to in order to succeed. Publishing both springs from and influences a culture, and an outsider can't easily participate in this subtle and nuanced interdependency.

In addition, the majority of a culture's publishing output is produced almost entirely for domestic consumption and therefore doesn't travel easily. Unlike commodities such as gasoline, clothing, cars, and furniture, published work developed for one country or culture needs extensive adaptation before it can enter a foreign market.

These cultural dependencies make international publishing a fascinating and challenging business. In spite of the highly focused nature of publishing, there are several compelling reasons why publishers need to work with international partners.

✧ Publishers in small markets can increase their sales tremendously by gaining access to larger overseas markets.

✧ Large and small publishers alike look to foreign markets for new ideas, innovation, technological improvement, and incremental revenue streams.

✧ Some publishing projects, though desirable and marketable, are simply not economical for a publisher in a small market to produce. In this case, adapting an existing publication from a publisher in a larger market may be the only option.

✧ International publishing is fun, exhilarating, and builds bridges between cultures.

These are the main drivers behind a vibrant and growing international publishing community.

This book provides a road map to the essential aspects of international publishing, from how to develop content that can be easily adapted to other cultures, to establishing relationships and negotiating licensing and co-publishing contracts. I discuss ways in which publishers can best reach foreign markets and how to reduce costs by working with overseas suppliers. Throughout the book I discuss the emergence of digital publishing and the challenges and opportunities provided by new technologies. The word "boundaries" in the book's title refers to the transition from print to electronic formats—which has, to some degree or another, impacted everyone in the publishing industry—as well as to cultural barriers and national borders.

This book is directed to a wide range of publishing professionals, whether they are in small, boutique publishing houses or large, multinational corporations. Experienced publishers should find the book useful if they have never worked in the international marketplace before or if they want to give their novice managers a firm grounding in best practices. For international rights managers, this book can serve as a blueprint to the various stages of the licensing process.

My experience over the past 28 years has been primarily in educational, nonfiction, and illustrated reference publishing. As a result, this book deals most directly with international publishing in these areas, where more steps are involved in bringing a product to market than simple translation (however artful), as would be the case in imaginative fiction or celebrity biography.

Educational publishers who develop large databases, multivolume publications, continuity series, multilevel programs, or collaborative work involving a variety of talents—from researching, writing, editing, and designing, to formatting and file converting—should find this book particularly relevant because it offers numerous ways for increasing resources while lowering costs as well as guidelines for internationalizing content. Anyone who wants to create or expand a publishing list will find this book useful.

The international marketplace can be an invaluable resource, a source of inspiration, and a destination for tapping into additional revenue streams. The global publishing community is made up of world citizens with a strong impulse to share information. Publishers, in general, are knowledge seekers, and knowledge has no boundaries. Knowing and seeing what other publishers around the world are doing is critical to creating relevant content that will be suitable for other markets. So it's important to attend international book fairs, to study what works in other markets, to develop an eye for products that might make sense in your market, and to contribute to the dissemination of useful knowledge—in other words, to join the community.

It's also important to see what forms or formats are being used in other markets and discover new channels for delivering content. Some of them may be relevant to your marketing plans while others may not be. But you may have content that other publishers want, either in its existing format or a different one that is more appropriate for their markets.

What happens in an international marketplace is an exchange of ideas, information, knowledge, creativity, and lifestyle that creates opportunities and establishes a community on a global scale. By taking advantage of them, you will be able to draw from a rich mine of content that will enhance your own publishing program. You should also find additional uses for your own content that may result in unplanned revenue streams. Publishing's final frontier—a fluid, innovative, global community—invites your active participation.

Chapter 1

Content for the Digital World

A lot has happened in the publishing community over the last five years. Many aspects of the business have seen dramatic changes. Most of these changes are the result of advances in electronic publishing and distribution. But due to the speed at which these changes have occurred and the variety of distribution channels that are now available, publishers have to alter the way in which they manage their products.

"Books have a clarity, visible authority and simplicity of use; online products have worldwide instant availability, infinite depth of search, and the appeal of television. The future lies in intelligent combination of the media that makes sense to consumers—a process we have scarcely begun."

--Ian Grant
Managing Director,
Britannica, U.K.

For most publishers the physical book is the paradigm of intellectual property. But that paradigm has been morphing into other forms as market forces require multiple types of deliveries, mostly in digital formats. So although the book (and other print-based products) is still a highly profitable, marketable, and useful (and perhaps the most intuitive) format, it is not the only one that people widely use. And, in the near future, it may not be the dominant one. Most of us already use a computer at the office or in school more than we use printed material. For this reason, it's important to be aware of various types of intellectual property other than print that can be produced, published, or licensed for a variety of purposes and in ways that print cannot accommodate. As we become increasingly accustomed to reading and getting our information in audio and video formats via laptops, phones, handhelds, and global positioning systems (GPS), the demand for high-quality intellectual property in flexible digital formats will increase dramatically.

Publishers have to think of themselves as producers of content rather than publishers of books or CD-ROMs or, for that matter, any other specific retrieval format. Their content should also be able to change form and format and move freely through a variety of channels. From the initial planning stages of a project to the production of final files, publishers have to consider multiple ways in which their content could be used, as well as specific issues related to intellectual property rights, so they can take full advantage of current and future distribution channels. Publishing today should be regarded as a continual process, not a one-time event.

The positive result of this process is the extended life span of a publication. Thanks to books-on-demand, and electronic publishing in general, books no longer have to go "out of print." They can be archived, accessed at any time in the future, and distributed more easily than ever before—and repurposed as the need or opportunity arises. We can now manage books and intellectual property with an eye toward keeping them in active circulation—either as a revised work, as part of a larger work, as a new book with a completely different design, or in a different format, such as a DVD or Web site.

Emerging Paradigms

Because of the growing number of devices that are used to transmit and obtain information, publishers need to think of intellectual property as "units" of information or content that can be linked together and then unlinked in multiple ways. These units can be treated individually in much the same way that an entire book can be and licensed separately from its original context. Given this new paradigm, we can take advantage of many types of traditional content that can be repurposed and reconfigured in any number of different places and in a variety of contexts. Text, databases, maps, music, audio, video, animations, illustrations, and computer code are all types of content that can be successfully licensed in whole or in part. Unbound from their original contexts, they become revenue-producing "intellectual property units" (IPUs). In this way, the individual parts of a final product may be worth more than the whole.

To illustrate this in the simplest way, we can view the photograph as perhaps the original IPU. Often the photographer does not know where a certain photo may end up, and a

"We're not in the book business; we're in the information business. Remember the great train lines of yesteryear? Neither do I, or anyone else, because they thought they were in the train business instead of the transportation business. We have to do two things: 1) Make our content available to our constituency in the form they really want; and 2) Find new customers/markets for our content, now that we've (hopefully) de-bound the book and have the content available in chunks."

--Sol Rosenberg
VP Marketing, Value
Chain International, Ltd.

single photo, perhaps taken with a specific intent in mind, can be used in a variety of different contexts over the course of many years. Photo agencies, such as Getty Images and Corbis, know very well the value of licensing and re-licensing a single photo and its ability to earn revenue over a long period of time without ever permanently leaving the owner's possession. All intellectual property should be viewed as IPUs with, if not evergreen, at least long-term earning potential. In short, with the ease of transmitting digital data, there is no reason why all types of content (text, music, maps, etc.) cannot follow the same model as the photograph.

With the flexibility provided by digital formats, content can be easily organized, assembled, disassembled, displayed, and accessed to be repurposed in different contexts and formats. This flexibility has been accelerated by the adoption of certain digital standards, which can make digital files readable and usable regardless of their origins. For example, with Extensible Markup Language (XML), text can be tagged and its structure clearly identified so that it can be used in Web documents and other electronic formats. Similarly, audio-video files should be compressed using the MPEG (Motion Picture Expert Group) standard. To make a product printer-ready, files should be converted to PDF (Portable Document Format), which converts any file, such as Windows, Macintosh, or Unix, into a common format for printing.

To be a successful publisher of digital content, you need to be prepared to expand or divide your content to meet market needs. This means that you have to think of your content as the culmination of carefully built, standardized electronic files. The reality is that today, the smallest common denominator for a valuable IPU is continually shrinking.

Making the Most Out of What You Make

Today, electronic publishing is an important part of every publisher's business plan in one way or another. At the very least, publishers are using Web sites to inform and update customers about their products and services, to provide shareholder information, or to recruit employees. Many publishers are also selling their products over the Web through e-commerce stores that they host themselves or co-brand with affiliates. Some publishers are using these Web sites as electronic storefronts in the same way that they use brick-and-mortar stores—for selling their physical products. Others are selling downloadable files derived directly from their books, either in PDF or one or more of the e-book formats. Because e-books are the most direct application of content transferred in its entirety from a non-digital format to a digital format, it's valuable to look at how this format has evolved.

E-books are very much what they sound like they are: books, mostly text only, downloaded from Web sites onto a computer and then transferred to, and accessed from, a proprietary viewer or reader. E-book downloads usually cost the same or slightly less than their equivalent softcover ink-on-paper versions, but still have comparatively low usage. I can't recall the last time I saw anyone using an e-book reader on the train or at the beach. However, they are likely to gain in popularity when a single standard format emerges. At the present time there are several available e-book formats, including readers from Adobe, Microsoft, Palm, and others, using various platforms—Windows, Macintosh, and Palm operating systems. The Adobe and Palm devices have the most cross-platform compatibility. There is momentum from the International Digital Publishing Forum (IDPF, formerly the Open eBook Forum) to settle on a single standard, but it's not entirely clear which format or formats will prevail, and there is no reason to bet on a particular horse at this point. Since publishers prepare their books for print publication in a digital format, there is no reason not to make the same content available as an e-book. Even if you are not prepared to sell e-books on your own Web site, there are plenty of e-book distributors—including the large online bookstores—that can manage this for you.

One of the reasons for the relatively slow growth of e-books, in addition to the multiple-format issue, is the convenience factor. It's not clear that an e-book has a great advantage over the printed book. Excluding the initial investment of the e-book device itself, single book titles cost about the same in print or as an e-book, they have more or less the same level of portability, and each has its strong points. An e-book reader has the advantage of being able to hold dozens of books; it can allow you to search for specific words or names; and it has the convenience of a built-in dictionary as well as other features, such as electronic bookmarks and sticky notes. On the other hand, a printed book doesn't require a separate device or batteries; it uses available light; it won't break, even if you drop it off of a hotel balcony; it can be inexpensively replaced; and, assuming you haven't lost or badly soiled it, it can be passed on to someone else. Electronic readers, however, don't require the death of a tree, which may or may not be a determining factor for some consumers. For publishers, if there is a lack of passion for e-books, it's simply because the economic case for e-books isn't compelling just yet.

Publish (electronically) or Perish

E-books aside, electronic publishing has dramatically affected the economics of most publishers. But it has had the most dramatic effect on publishers of large databases, who have been forced to make substantial changes in the ways in which they produce, market, and distribute their publications. For reference publishers whose products draw from an ever-expanding database or multiple databases, there are market-driving advantages to their electronic offerings over their traditional print counterparts.

Today, large multivolume reference works are more expensive in print than the same content in electronic form, and they are not as portable. Printed and bound, they can't be updated as frequently. In order to have the new and revised content in print, the original product has to be replaced in its entirety, which is neither economical nor convenient since it's likely that only a relatively small percentage of the content was (or needed to be) updated. Annual supplements have attempted to serve as a more economical way of updating a large set of books without abandoning the base product, but these volumes usually do a better job of summarizing the prior year's events than keeping an entire set of books current.

With the use of good indexes, finding information is certainly not difficult in print. But customized, professionally compiled indexes—which are excellent at mapping topics, showing relationships, and pointing the user to related content—are not as effective as search engines for quickly finding specific information. While print reference works are aesthetically appealing when lavishly illustrated and composed in a well-designed layout, they cannot contain (without supplements) multimedia elements—such as video, animations, interactivities, and music—which are compelling enhancements of most electronic reference products.

Print reference works have several excellent qualities as well as real advantages over their electronic equivalents, which is why there still is a viable global market for them. They don't require hardware and software to access; they remain accessible at all times and in perpetuity; they can provide a more satisfying browsing experience; they are easier to read; and several volumes can be opened at once in order to compare and contrast subjects or for use by more than one user.

Yet with inexpensive (and sometimes free) versions of these same products available on CDs and DVDs, and the low cost of monthly and annual subscriptions to their online versions, it's not difficult to see why the market for general and specialized electronic encyclopedias and references has grown dramatically over the last five years while the market for these same products in print form has declined. If you already own or have access to a computer, which most everyone does (if only through schools and public libraries), the value proposition for the electronic version over the print version of reference works is easy to make.

As long as it is economical to do so, publishers need to be able to provide their content in as many formats as the market demands. For some products, both print and (various) electronic versions may continue to co-exist. For other products, it's possible that only the electronic versions will be sustainable, in spite of some of the advantages that print may offer. Market forces will determine which formats will prevail in the long run. My main point here is that it's the content—the intellectual property—that offers the greatest value, not the particular format it is in. If publishers are not already doing so, they need to be prepared to provide their content in the formats that will be required tomorrow. If they do, there is probably already a growing market to tap into today.

The Economics of Electronic Content

Marketing models for electronic content are continuing to evolve, but there are now a variety of ways for publishers to generate revenue from electronic content. Publishers with substantial databases—key content providers—are successfully selling their online products and services, either in part or whole, on a subscription basis, often by the year or month and sometimes for even shorter time periods. For some consumer or niche information services, such as product-rating services, even "day passes" are common. For consumers, this is a good way to experience the value of a service when they need it without having to make a long-term commitment. For the content provider, this kind of short-term, small-revenue trial, or micro-charge, helps to build customer loyalty and good will.

Another viable model for distributing digital content to consumers is to take advantage of Digital Rights Management (DRM) technology. This involves encrypting the code with a digital expiration date so that the rights to the content terminate and the product itself, in essence, becomes unavailable. This is a very good way for software, music, and video publishers to license their content to those who may want to have an extended trial of an application or product before they decide to buy it or simply don't feel that they can benefit from having the program or file as a permanent part of their collection. It's commonly used in academic institutions that may require certain videos, for example, as part of a course offering but don't see a permanent value in owning them. DRM content is priced at a substantial discount over the full ownership price, but it can also be licensed with an option to buy.

As traffic over the Web continues to grow, and as advertising, subscription, DRM, and other models demonstrate that they can provide more than just incremental profit, publishers will be looking to enhance their online offerings with better and, when possible, exclusive content. Another advantage of digital content is that you don't have to pre-determine what content people will want. The economics of digital publishing allows you to make it all available so that the market can choose.

Getting to the Good Stuff

There is growing evidence that individuals and businesses are willing to pay for quality content. And there are several good reasons for this. With the dramatic increase in the number of Web sites, free as well as subscription sites, it is becoming more difficult to distinguish quality sites from amateur or inferior sites just by randomly searching the Web. The most popular search engines, such as Ask, Yahoo, Google and others, make this process of quality differentiation even more difficult in several ways. First, they favor sites that pay them for higher placements in the search results pages through the competitive selling of text and graphical advertising via keywords—the most popular keywords going to the highest bidders. Also, because of the way search-engine algorithms work, the more links a content site gets from other sites, the higher that site will appear on the search engine results page and the lower the SERP (search engine ranking position) will be. For this reason, the very best content may not always rise to the top.

"Users have access to (more and more varied) information from a wide variety of competing sources 24/7. And the means of access to this information continue to change . . . more and more rapidly. Sources that sometimes seem to be reputable are not."

--Ellen R. Bialo
President, IESD, Inc.

In this environment consumers will seek out sites that they know and trust, either from their experience with a brand's offline products and services or from its most current offerings online. Experienced and non-experienced online users alike will naturally turn to brands that they can associate with authority and accuracy and that have earned their trust by having been tested over time and, increasingly, as the brands have migrated to other media. As a result, Web sites across a broad spectrum of market channels will demand higher quality content.

To respond to this need, publishers can create content from scratch or they can license what they need from other publishers. Most publishers are doing both now. The challenge is to build brand and major revenue streams by providing content directly to users that has the highest possible value proposition and, at the same time, to license, if possible, quality content to other publishers that does not compromise, or conflict with, this primary objective.

Wrapping Things Up

Why one electronic application works better in some markets than in others is a function of culture, lifestyle, trends, and sometimes the inexplicable. If you are a content provider, however, as opposed to a change-agent in a market, the most important thing you can do is be prepared to respond to market demand—and then find the right partner to help you get to the market and sustain your market position.

In order to have an electronic strategy that is going to work in as many markets as possible, publishers need to be flexible and willing to adapt to rapidly changing market requirements. Above all, publishers need to think of themselves as format-neutral and be prepared to be cross-format or multi-format providers. What's important is the quality of the content and its suitability for various markets, regardless of the delivery system. After that, marketing success will depend on strong relationships with partners who understand their particular market dynamics.

Try This!

The opportunities are almost infinite for taking slices of your content or database and licensing them for use in other products and channels. Consider having someone in your organization dedicated to this activity, and seek out opportunities anywhere that your content can add value.

Chapter 2

Publish Locally, Publish Globally

I t stands to reason that you first have to master the nuances of your own market—and publish according to the standards expected of high-quality publications that appeal to your primary audience—before you can begin to think about making products that will be successful in other countries with different cultures, tastes, and, in many cases, a different language. But if you are designing your products from the outset so that they will also be appropriate for an international audience, you should keep a few basic guidelines in mind throughout the development process. By paying attention to some fundamental editorial and design principles, you will be able to improve the ability of someone else to leverage your products successfully in another culture. You will not only make your products more appealing to other publishers, but you will also make their job of adapting and marketing them easier.

These guidelines are not meant to be all-inclusive; as examples of do's and don'ts they should be relevant enough to apply to most situations. At the same time, even though these are not the only issues that you will need to consider, I have tried to focus on what I know to be well-tested strategies. They should need only a minimum amount of adaptation for your publishing projects—depending on the subject matter and the intended age and interest of the audience for your products—and should give you a good framework for the kind of planning necessary to make your products as appealing as possible to an overseas publisher.

Using Universal References, Illustrations, and Examples

Whenever we are introducing a new topic or subject, trying to make a point as clear as possible, or drawing a comparison between disparate things, we often need to use examples or references. Visual or descriptive examples naturally come from our own experiences and culture—especially colorful and vivid ones—but they sometimes run the risk of being too limited to our own culture and frame of reference to have the impact that we intend when adapted or translated into another culture or context. Although it is natural to rely on the things that are most familiar to us and our audience when using references to illustrate a concept or to make a point, it is important, especially for a global publishing community, to make our examples as universal as possible. In fact, with a little thought it is often just as easy to make the same point even more interesting and meaningful by using an example that could be easily understood by almost anyone.

For example, Smokey Bear may serve as a colorful and memorable symbol for emphasizing the danger of forest fires and how important it is to prevent them, but few people outside of North America are familiar with Smokey. If you are publishing a book on forest preservation, a topic with global appeal, Smokey should probably not appear in it, even though he would immediately come to mind to an American author or educator. By being vigilant in filtering out these kinds of culture traps you will make your publications easier to adapt for other cultures. Here are a few areas where this strategy will apply.

When developing an illustrated product, especially one on a general interest topic such as nature, science, or geography, you should try to look for images from outside of North America whenever possible. For example, if you are talking generally about lakes or mountains, try to use well-known landmarks from the U.K. or Switzerland instead of Minnesota or Arizona. If you are showing street scenes or bridges, be sure to select foreign destinations as well as places close to home. If you need to show a natural phenomenon or even a natural disaster, go outside of the Western Hemisphere in search of an example. Floods occur almost everywhere in the world—frequently, unfortunately, in India, Thailand, and the Philippines—not just along the banks of the Mississippi. Using examples from many regions of the world reflects positively on the relevance of the content for a broad spectrum of people.

Regardless of where we live in the world, we share more things in common than there are differences between us. Even so, we don't do things identically. People celebrate holidays or play sports, study, and work together everywhere on the planet. Look beyond your own backyard when showing common, everyday human activities and experiences. Your efforts will pay off not just in relevance and appeal to foreign markets, but in intrinsic value as well. A publication that takes more of the world into consideration is, at its core, a more interesting and important work.

"To be successful in local markets, ideally I need people who speak the local language, know the local business culture, are trustworthy and understand my business needs."

--Sebastian Gutmann Gutmann+Gutmann, Germany

Avoid highly culture-bound examples, such as Thanksgiving or the Fourth of July. Use universal concepts that either everyone will understand or that can be easily adapted. When it comes to using sports as an example, choose soccer (called football most everywhere else), or basketball if you can, instead of American (or Australian) football or baseball.

If your content contains measurements, be sure to make accommodations for the metric system or, in the case of temperature, Celsius as well as Fahrenheit. If you are developing science content and illustrating electrical systems, be sure to note that electrical outlets look different in other countries. (There's a reason for those A.C. adapters sold at international airports.)

Depicting cars could cause a problem depending on what side of the road people drive on, since it will affect which side of the car the steering wheel is on. License plates differ from country to country, and this too can be an immediate indicator of place, which is fine if it's intentional and essential for the context.

You will also want to avoid showing signs and billboards since place names, language, and advertising that appear on them can limit the mobility of content.

When publishing photos of people young and old, you should show them from diverse backgrounds and from a variety of cultures. This is an easy thing to do, it costs you no more, and it makes your product travel better. It also shows a sensitivity that is critical in international publishing. Bring the community in, and the community will recognize and embrace one of its own.

Specific animals also can present a problem. Cows are sacred in India, for example, so certain depictions of them may cause problems. Pigs, as well, require special treatment in some places. Some birds and animals are found only in certain climates, so how they are used and portrayed should take the local geography into consideration. I once got into an argument with a publishing partner in the U.K. over the use of a rooster in an illustration. His claim was that so few British children are exposed to roosters that they shouldn't be shown in a farm scene. To me, that seemed like an excellent argument in favor of showing the rooster. Still, it points to the issue of how closely sense and meaning are tied to familiar objects, even in situations where you may not anticipate a problem.

Seasons are not as straightforward as they might seem. Not everyone experiences all four of them in the same way, and winter doesn't always mean snow and below zero (Celsius or Fahrenheit) temperatures. Also, half the planet has summer while the other half has winter. What may seem like simple things to depict—a "typical" fall or winter scene, for example—depends entirely on what side of the Equator you live on.

Geo-publishing

Maps are a special problem—one that you should anticipate—and present their own unique set of considerations. This is because there are a handful of high-profile, hotly contested boundary and territory disputes in such places as India and Pakistan over Kashmir; Greece over the name of the Republic of Macedonia (FYROM—Former Yugoslav Republic of Macedonia—is what they, and the U.N., call it); Korea and Japan over two tiny islands about halfway between them—Dokdo to the Koreans, Takeshima to the Japanese; and China over Taiwan and Tibet, as just a few examples.

Although you are generally on solid editorial ground for most markets if you use the United Nations' official designations for geographical locations and boundaries, it won't satisfy the countries listed here unless you label these "contested" territories their way. (And in some cases, such as Macedonia, the U.N. will differ from a particular nation's, as well as the U.S. State Department's, official name.) In fact, when it comes to Chinese maps, you may even have a problem using printers in China if boundaries are not shown according to China's conventions. Vendors are instructed to make the "necessary" changes on their own, often at the dismay of the publishers.

If you can't avoid showing these problem places on maps because the content requires it, make sure that you have established an editorial policy that you can clearly communicate, and stick to it. However, if you are flexible and can allow the target market's position to drive some of your editorial decisions, you will be in the best position to license your products. If your editorial policy is to label your maps—regardless of the language and the market—according to U.N. conventions, then you may run into problems getting past censors in certain countries. The choice is up to you. Although I can't say definitively what the right thing to do is, you need to be aware of your options and have a plan. The following "Case in Point" is how we handled one of these situations.

A Case in Point

We had a publishing partner who was adapting one of our multivolume series that had maps scattered throughout the volumes. We ran into a problem when we could not agree on how to label some of the controversial territories. Certain names that the publisher wanted to use on the maps would have conflicted with our in-house editorial policy, and we didn't want our brand on a product that contained what we considered to be incorrect map labels. The solution was to put the maps in a separate atlas volume, label the maps according to the publisher's standards, and remove our branding from that one volume. In this way the maps didn't disrupt the editorial integrity of the project and gave the publisher the marketing flexibility they needed.

Early Detection

The solutions that you and your publishing partners come up with will depend entirely on the nature of the problems, your ability to raise these problems as early in the process as possible, and your willingness to compromise—internally and externally. In the case cited above, we had to convince our editorial department that the compromise we made to be successful in this market did not jeopardize our editorial integrity.

Global politics aside, especially as they might apply to cartographic issues, you can and should avoid parochialism whenever you get the chance. The opportunity to do so is greater than you might think—or at least greater perhaps than your staff might think. What matters in the end is not just what you know or what you are conscious of, but what your staff is capable of doing on your behalf. It is critical that your entire development team be part of the diversifying effort. This may sound obvious, but if you don't make a point of it, and if it's not ingrained in the development process, it won't happen.

Organizing Principles

It is much easier to license a product that is organized thematically rather than alphabetically. Since the spelling of terms differs from language to language, even from British English to American English, alphabetically arranged products have to be completely rearranged based on the target language spelling. This could provide a barrier to licensing simply because the licensee now has to consider the costs of changing the layouts and re-indexing in addition to translating, adapting, and localizing the content by adding new material relevant to the target market.

Thematically arranged products, on the other hand, can stay in the same sequence when translated into another language and can usually take advantage of the existing design and layout. If the design is appealing and suitable for other markets, the licensee can retain the existing layout, make full use of the color elements, and translate and adapt only the text pages, or black plate. Even with a fully digital production process, where film has been completely eliminated, it still saves time and costs to retain as much of the original design as possible—even if random photos or illustrations need to be changed. It's still better than having to restructure the product completely.

In addition, if the entire design and layout with all of the color elements in place can be identical for more than one language—with the only difference being the black plates—then there is the chance that the printing of multiple language versions can be ganged, or printed at the same time, saving money and providing better margins for each publishing partner. A thematically organized product that requires only black-plate changes offers the best opportunity for taking advantage of the creative elements of the original publication as well the ability to achieve economies of scale when it's time to go to press. Of course, after the first printing, assuming that individual sales efforts in different markets did not deplete the stock of all languages at the same rate, it may not be practical to gang multiple languages at press time. But at least the option will be there.

If your business plan calls for your product to be translated into other languages, be sure to put 100% of the text elements into the black plate, and avoid putting even captions or titles in color or reversing them out of white. Even though you will be transferring the finished product in the form of electronic files rather than film—which is basically the only option you have today—you still want to make the adaptation process as easy as possible and leave all printing options open. This is not a technical issue; it's a design issue. And there is no reason why doing this has to detract from an attractive and innovative design.

For every edict, there is an exception. So although the value of making only black-plate changes holds true for most languages, the benefit isn't as great for some other languages—such as Chinese, Japanese, Hebrew, or Arabic where the layouts will have to be reversed, for starters, since the reading conventions for these languages go from right to left, not left to right. But there is still the benefit of not having to shuffle every page and to be able to work instead with fully composed spreads.

If you intend to develop a product for co-publishing and licensing, be sure that your design allows for additional space in the text areas that will be needed for both Asian and European languages. For example, German normally takes up to 15% more space than English does. So your design should have enough white space around the text to accommodate more lines per page. Some Asian languages will require even more space. Malaysian, for example, may require up to 40% more space, so it's probably not practical to have a design that works equally well in Malaysian and, say, French. The point here is to make sure that your design is not so cluttered with media and your text so dense that the product would have to be completely redone for foreign markets. It's easier to plan for this in advance than to find out later that the design might cause your partner to make unnecessary editorial compromises or to abandon the project entirely.

Clearing Rights

If your product includes third-party photos, be sure to clear worldwide rights in all formats, electronic and print, and in all languages whenever possible. By doing so, you won't have to negotiate for these rights after you have made a licensing deal.

Buying photo rights used to be a very expensive, laborious, and frustrating task. There was little or no consistency among photo stock agencies and independent photographers regarding their pricing policies or the rights that they were prepared to grant. In spite of the fact that the supply of photos has historically exceeded the demand, agencies were able to charge exorbitant prices and grant only limited rights—restricted territories, one language at a time, and for a short-term limit. And if you dealt with dozens of photo agencies or independent photographers, managing the assets from these sources, along with the various terms and conditions that came with them, was a time-consuming and costly task.

Over the last few years, however, the process of licensing photos has become far easier to manage and the costs for buying extended rights in multiple formats and languages have declined dramatically. As a result, today there is no reason not to buy as broad of rights as you might need upfront, so you can eliminate any possible issue surrounding the use of photos or the question of what rights are available, and in which territories, when you are negotiating a licensing deal.

In spite of the consolidation in the photo licensing business—with several large photo stock agencies, such as Associated Press, Corbis, and Getty Images being the dominant suppliers—there is a huge supply of photos available on the market and a willingness by the agencies to make it easier for publishers to find and select the photos they need and to adjust their pricing to fit the publishers' cost structures. In addition, thanks to the Web, it's easier to access what once was difficult-to-find or unique photography and to acquire images at extremely favorable rates. The ability to first view then download image files via the Web has also reduced dramatically the physical costs of photo re-licensing, especially from overseas suppliers.

What used to be a seller's market (because of control, not short supply) is now a buyer's market, and photo agencies can no longer demand a premium for their images; nor can they easily charge incremental fees for extended rights, such as additional languages, territories, or formats. Today, one reasonable fee should cover all the rights you need.

Many photo agencies now also have subscription services available where, for a monthly fee, you can have unlimited use of all the photos from selected collections. The rights you get for photos chosen from these services are the same as if you bought the photos individually—typically life of a print or CD/DVD product and 7 to 10 years online.

Although some negotiation is still required, most types of photography—from the larger stock agencies—can be acquired for editorial uses under these longer term limits and multiple formats and languages for around U.S. $100 **or less** per photo, depending on the quantity of photos you purchase within a specified period of time. You can often get images from independent photographers or individuals for far less than that. However, there are still exceptions. Rare or hard-to-find photos and fine arts images, where artists' rights are involved in addition to agency fees, often require special negotiation. And sometimes, depending on the rights owner, there is little wiggle room.

As an alternative model, large agencies will provide some of their photo collections on a royalty-free basis, which means that you may pay slightly more up front for a photo, but once you license it, you can use it in perpetuity in any of your publications without any restrictions or further payment. Royalty-free photos become part of your asset collection.

Unless you need images for very specific editorial content, you will find that there are plenty of quality sites, such as the Library of Congress and non-profit associations, from which you can get a wide variety of photos on a broad spectrum of subjects at very reasonable rates. Some of these places, like NASA, tourist agencies, city (or country) chambers of commerce, and publicity departments of large corporations will provide photos for free or for a nominal transfer fee.

Overall, the cost of buying photo rights is a fraction of what it was just five years ago, or at least it should be if you are approaching the right suppliers and you know what the current market conditions are. You should take advantage of what has become a fundamental shift in the business environment and acquire photo rights as broadly as possible and for as long of a term as possible—and make it easy for your potential partners to license your product without having to clear photo rights. They still may have to replace or add a certain percentage of photos to account for new local content, but at least they won't have to worry about the photos that are already placed in the product.

Standardizing Formats

Part of the licensing process includes providing production files so that the licensee can make any necessary changes prior to arranging for printing or posting in a viewable electronic format. In order to make sure that this part of the process goes smoothly, whether you are working with a partner in parallel markets or in foreign markets, it is important that your files be available in standard digital file formats, such as XML (Extensible Markup Language) to accommodate any electronic format, and Quark or Adobe InDesign for page layout and design. You will also need to transfer these files either on discs or post them on an FTP (File Transfer Protocol) site. This is a password-protected site, which you should set up and host, from where your licensees can download text and image files.

In short, content must be as easy as possible to license from a technical point of view. Text, images, photographs, and videos should not only be in standard digital formats, but also should be tagged and indexed so that you can find specific content quickly. If your content includes multimedia elements, be sure to keep your various audio and image files separate for easy translation, editing, or replacement. This means that you have to work closely with your information technology (IT) department so that your content is ready to travel when the deal is complete.

A good asset management system is invaluable for identifying and keeping track of content as you add elements to your databases and as you license portions of it to partners. There are numerous options available including Web-based and open-source software that will allow you to do this. There is continuous innovation in this area, so examine what's available carefully in order to identify the right system for your purposes. Consider an application that can be adapted to meet different needs as your content licensing activity evolves and becomes more meaningful to your P&L. At the same time, you should not acquire more features than you need until you are certain that licensing content slices is going to be more than just something you do when someone comes to you with a request. It has to be part of your overall strategy and a publishing activity to which you devote adequate resources. But if you have valuable content that can be used in a variety of different contexts, an asset management system will likely pay off.

Slicing and Dicing

The number of digital outlets for quality content is growing worldwide. Web sites, especially in multiple languages for international markets, represent one channel for licensing content or content modules. In addition, the opportunities are growing in both cable and wireless delivery systems for customized content, which is often presented differently from its original format and intent. Content providers now have access to a variety of channels for licensing content, on a non-exclusive basis, to traditional and non-traditional publishers and distributors who can successfully market portions of the same content in an entirely distinct context for a specific market segment.

"The biggest change we've seen is the technical change—computers for design and the use of email, Web sites, etc. We struggle to keep up with this—financially and skills—but obviously it has made life much easier: smoother and cheaper production processes and much better communication. Our 'in house' team all work in different places in the U.K. and communicate with each other and with our customers and suppliers as if we were in the same building. . . .We need better IT skills so we can send material electronically through FTP sites and email."

--*Catherine Bruzzone Publisher, b small publishing, U.K.*

The key to licensing of this type, if you are the licensor, is to make sure that you don't cannibalize your own products or markets. As long as you are careful as to what you license and to whom you license it—and that by licensing you are confident that you are reaching a market that you wouldn't normally be able to reach—licensing part of your assets becomes an excellent strategy for monetizing sunk development costs.

This strategy is particularly relevant in foreign markets and, especially, in other languages. The chances of cannibalization decrease substantially as you migrate your content into other languages. In fact, unless you plan on translating and delivering the content yourself in foreign markets, the risks of cannibalization approach zero. For this reason, it's important to make this type of licensing a priority, especially if you have unique content that can be separated into distinct elements, such as media on a specific subject, statistical information, or any content that can be used in several different contexts.

Licensing content should not be restricted to any one medium. The same strategy applies equally well to print and electronic delivery. The key here is being able to catalog and make available the assets that you have built up over time so that they can be used in any format—print, online, CD/DVD, and even handheld devices.

Wireless technology is becoming more accessible as well as inexpensive, and manufacturers are increasingly using quality content as a way to differentiate their products. This technology will be demanding more content for a wide range of demographics, and for a variety of purposes, including homework help, test assessment, hotel and restaurant selection, traffic information, and directions. With the increasing innovation going on in this field, your electronic strategy considerations should include how your content could be made applicable and relevant to wireless users.

In the international environment, you will discover that different markets have adopted or embraced different technologies. In some markets you will be surprised at how far-reaching and entrenched wireless applications have already become, whereas in other markets you might find entrenched technologies that are basically obsolete here. All of this is good news for the content provider. It represents opportunities to license content in different formats.

In some countries, such as Japan, Korea, Singapore, and the Philippines, wireless and broadband technologies have merged faster in consumer applications than they have in North America. At Britannica, for example, we've been able to license content to large consumer electronic publishers in Japan and Korea that offer handheld devices that are simply not available in North America or Europe. Some of these are wireless devices with online access to databases and others are basically standalone electronic "libraries."

"Our clients struggle with many areas, but the one that they seem to find most challenging is keeping pace with how information/product is delivered to users."

*--Ellen R. Bialo
President, IESD, Inc.*

Licensing Benefits and Caveats

Keeping in mind that digital content can take on a variety of shapes and formats, let's look at how both a licensee and licensor can benefit from licensing content, as well as what some of the caveats might be.

For a licensee, acquiring content from someone else provides quick access to content that might otherwise be difficult, time-consuming, and/or costly to develop. The licensee must determine that licensing content will save both time and money and perhaps take advantage of the reputation of the licensor, assuming that the content provider is both a credible source and a brand that is readily recognized in the marketplace. Also, there is the opportunity to forge a new relationship and an ongoing source of quality content.

However, for a licensee, there are downsides to licensing content. Normally a content provider will not let you license content on an exclusive basis, which means that you are unlikely to gain a complete market advantage with that particular content. Also, there is generally a term limit on how long the license will last without additional payments. And licensed material usually cannot be sub-licensed by the licensee, which restricts you to the defined use for which you are licensing the content. So although licensing content is often faster and cheaper than starting from scratch, it has its limitations.

Therefore, when you are considering whether to license content, make sure that you are not sacrificing a strategic advantage. If you think that you may be at a high risk of doing so, then you should consider taking the time and investing the resources necessary to create the content yourself—and own it. When you're leasing content, try to make sure of the following:

✧ That you need it for a specific purpose;

✧ That you will be granted as broad of a license as necessary to cover your channels;

✧ That the content fills a somewhat narrow purpose, such as a niche or non-core content area;

✧ That it will save substantial money over the cost of original development; and

✧ That you are prepared to take the risk that at some time in the future you might either lose the license (and have to re-license it) or find another source for the same content.

Above all, make sure that the content you are licensing is not identifiable with your core competence. If it is, you should probably build it yourself and make it a permanent part of your portfolio.

For a licensor, there may be several benefits to licensing content, particularly for small slices of content that are largely disassociated from their primary or original context. First and foremost, licensing generates incremental revenue. Further, if the content is branded, the brand can benefit from the additional exposure to new markets and customers. It's also an opportunity to develop new alliances and partnerships and, at the same time, pre-empt competitors from licensing similar content from someone else.

There are, of course, some prudent guidelines for maximizing the upside and minimizing the downside of licensing your valuable IPU:

✦ The content should be able to be licensed with as little customizing as possible;

✦ You should make sure that you own the content outright and that it is not encumbered—by royalties or agents' fees—in any way;

✦ The licensed product will represent your brand well; and

✦ Above all, when licensed the content will cause no, or insignificant, channel conflict with your main business activities.

Wrapping Things Up

Taking the necessary steps to prepare your content properly for adaptation at the beginning of the development process is much easier than trying to make accommodations after the fact. Moreover, you can make your product adaptable in other languages and cultures without changing the quality or character of the content, or compromising its original intent. It should be no less marketable in your primary market by making minor adjustments for an international audience, and it will have a greater chance of becoming a valuable asset in a different culture.

If care is taken to create a product so that it can meet the needs of local markets with a minimum amount of adaptation, it is more likely to be licensed and successfully marketed. If you design your product with this kind of care and attention to local detail, it differentiates your product from competitive products and becomes a marketing advantage. The details of how well the product is "internationalized" should be spelled out in a specification sheet and made part of the marketing messages as you present your product to potential partners. You should indicate, in as much detail as possible, the various ways in which the product has been created to make adaptation and translation easy and effective so that the licensed product doesn't look like it originated from a "foreign" source. The most successful products are those that appear to be locally produced rather than merely translated or adapted from another language and culture.

Try This!

In order to understand how best to maximize the value of your product in other cultures, consider working with a sensitivity expert, especially for your main overseas markets. Get this input at the beginning of a project, and allow time for adequate review in the development schedule.

Chapter 3

What's in a Name?

As is the case in all kinds of consumer marketing, brand equity will make a big difference in your ability to sell or license your products. Having said that, it's important to recognize exactly how much preference a brand might be given in a specific category of publishing. For example, we know that Disney is a recognized world brand that appeals to similar demographics in many cultures; and it's been an excellent brand for building successful licensees, not just in videos, games, and toys but in the publishing world as well. The Disney brand is often a preferred (if not insisted upon) brand, especially when used for products aimed at young children. We can find the Disney brand on a wide range of books and CDs for kids, in dozens of languages. Many publishers license the Disney brand to help sell their own locally produced content—from coloring books to high-end picture books. As with all successful global branding strategies, the Disney brand is promoted differently depending on the language and culture while satisfying strict corporate licensing guidelines.

Book licensing for companies like Disney, Lucas Films, Warner Bros., or Pixar, to name a few of the true mega-brands, is not only a very big business—it's basically an industry in itself. At the same time, there are some publishing areas in which these successful, global brands may not be as valuable as in others. Except for very young children in a few Asian markets, educational licensing, for example, is not one of Disney's most active or successful publishing categories. Nor does the Disney brand play as well in reference publishing as, say, Britannica, National Geographic, the BBC, or the Discovery Channel. With this in mind, if you are a publisher in Korea, you might be better off with the Merriam-Webster brand than, say, Nintendo if you wanted to produce a line of dictionaries, even for young people.

Brand Alignment

Whether you are the licensor or the licensee, it's important to align the brand with a category of publishing with which it can be easily associated. If you want to differentiate a line of activity books for three- and four-year-olds, you might want to license the Crayola or Lego brand or build a product around Warner Bros. cartoon characters. Conversely, you probably wouldn't use Crayola on a new series of history books for middle school. It's the wrong target age group, for starters, and it doesn't have the appropriate resonance for the subject area. The History Channel would probably be a better bet for educational content aimed at that age level. As an example of good brand alignment, Dorling Kindersley (DK), a children's illustrated-reference publisher, used the global Lego brand very successfully in a line of high-interest graded readers based on Lego themes, such as exploring space or seizing a castle. These educational books combine DK text and design with photography of characters and structures made from Lego blocks. The two brands align well because DK is a highly regarded educational publisher, and the Lego Company stands for creativity and innovation worldwide.

The mega-brands mentioned above are examples of global brands with unusually strong equity. These brands are recognized as leaders in their fields and carry a lot of customer trust that has been tested over time and often across cultures. Any one of them, though not associated directly with educational publishing, could be used on educational products. They just have to be correctly aligned with the right demographics. Because of their name recognition, they have the ability to create opportunities in a variety of market segments that would not be available to other entities.

However, in various niche-publishing categories, there are lesser-known yet high-value "brands," many of which can have a meaningful impact in their specialty markets and can help build customer loyalty. These are small- and medium-sized companies that are well respected in their area of specialization—in some cases even across languages—but are not familiar consumer brands like Disney or Warner Bros. In fact, there are only a handful of brands that ever attain that same level of name recognition. But educational companies such as Larousse and Universalis in France, Langensheit in Germany, Merriam-Webster in the U.S., and Bloomsbury in the U.K. all have brands that, in their publishing segments, have the potential to perform better than these mega-brands.

If you are licensing products and have a brand that is well known in your market segment, it's important to recognize its value and use it to your advantage. At the same time, if you are shopping for books to license, try to discover brands that have equity value in other cultures and leverage them. You might be helped in ways that you had not anticipated, especially if the brand you work with suddenly comes up with a hit in a different consumer segment and gives your publishing efforts an unexpected boost. Pokémon, which began as a card game, and Thomas and Friends, featuring Thomas the Tank Engine, are two such examples, and have helped to spin off a large number of successful books and digital products. Michelin, for many years, has been another brand that has had great success with its publishing programs, and remains as one of the standards in the travel book business, even though its core business is the manufacturing and selling of tires.

The key to a real brand coup, of course, is to select a brand that has not yet become world famous. If you are lucky (or prophetic) enough to pick a brand before it becomes well known, you might be able to take advantage of the brand's growing momentum in the marketplace before it becomes too expensive to leverage. If the brand has not yet reached its zenith, the cost of entry will be much lower. For obvious reasons, with a half a dozen titles, millions of books in dozens of languages, movies, and countless brand spin-offs having already saturated the world market, now would not be the best time to begin to take advantage of the Harry Potter phenomenon. It's probably too late to get any value out of it, especially for additional book derivatives. At this point, you would be paying too high of a premium to leverage that brand. Of course, trying to find the next Harry Potter, before it's already a household name, is everyone's goal.

Brand Extension

Once you venture outside of the mega-brands—world-class marks that are established in a variety of consumer segments—it is possible to find real opportunity with category brands. Universities, for example, especially Harvard, Cambridge, Princeton, Wharton, and Oxford, have done an excellent job of extending their brands and making them relevant in other publishing areas.

Associations and not-for-profits, such as the International Reading Association (IRA) and the American Medical Association (AMA), have been very effective in extending their brands based on their reputation among their members and the influence they have outside of their organizations. One of the best examples, both in the U.S. and the U.K., are their respective automotive associations, AAA and AA.

Corporations and celebrities have also been able to leverage the trust that their brands have built in the minds of consumers to generate easily recognized publications. Campbell's Soup, Kraft Foods, General Mills through its Betty Crocker brand, Martha Stewart, Rachael Ray, and Wolfgang Puck have spawned numerous cook books; Home Depot and Black and Decker have licensed their brand for home repair books; and Microsoft recently announced a series of executive training books that will be published by John Wiley & Sons.

These are only a few examples of corporate icons that have used their name recognition and credibility to partner with publishers. Two things in particular are accomplished. The corporations get additional branding and marketing—in a sense free advertising—in addition to royalty revenue generated from the publications. The publisher, or licensee, gets to leverage the brand to help accelerate sales. The idea is that the corporate brands are not only well recognized and respected, but they are also positively associated with the content of the publications. The branding association helps to differentiate the content of one publisher over another.

Brand extension, like brand alignment, must be well managed and applied carefully so that it is not abused. Customers not only trust the brand, but they must be able to feel that they can trust this particular application or extension of the brand. The brand extension must be logical and well directed and cannot be seen as a stretch. If so, the market will reject it. As a hypothetical example, it probably would not be a good idea if McDonalds were to put its name on a line of software products or for IBM, on the other hand, to help McDonalds sell burgers with a "McPC meal." In reality,

"The most important thing to consider in finding a partner overseas [is] to find a business partner, well-established in the market, whose ambitions in a three- to five-year timeframe complement one's own. Few partnerships last longer. Accept the fact that markets and people will change."

--Ian Grant
Managing Director,
Britannica, U.K.

I remember a well-loved cereal brand that failed completely when it tried to use its brand on educational workbooks and Web sites. Why did it fail? Cereal cannot bridge the divide between pure fun and education, whereas Lego, as indicated above—with its clear association with skills, architecture, engineering, and design—can.

Wrapping Things Up

Although brands can be huge assets in establishing immediate intimacy with customers and gaining market share, not all brands, even the most recognized ones, play equally in all markets. It's possible that, in certain markets, your partner may actually have a better brand than you do. This goes back to the power of local publishing. The goal is to win market share, and you will have the greatest chance of doing this by leading with the best brand, whether it's yours or your partner's.

You and your partner share the same goal, so you should be able to agree on how to reach it. If your partner feels that your content in his market will be more effective with different branding, then your best option is to defer to your partner. If you are not convinced, you can always get this verified independently by conducting focus groups with local marketing and branding agencies. In the end, you will need to rely on the judgment of your partner. This may require swallowing some pride on the one hand and making a leap of faith on the other. By relying on some basic market analysis and sticking to the plan, you and your partner will come to the logical and right conclusion without getting into a battle of the brands.

Try This!

It's a good idea to have your brand tested in another market by a local research group. Even if you have a well-known brand, it will resonate differently in different markets. The data you get from an independent group will be invaluable if you want to test your brand against a potential partner's or if you want to find out how you can build your brand in a new market.

Chapter 4

Where Publishers Meet

The primary business of international publishing is the buying and selling of books and content in one form or another. If you are a publisher who has built up a sizable list of publications, you may want to find someone to license or distribute your content in order to further leverage the investment that you have made in developing your product line. On the other hand, if you want to supplement your existing portfolio quickly without heavily investing in developing new products from the ground up (or even start a new product line), you will probably be interested in locating a publisher who has compatible products from whom you can acquire content.

Either way, whether you are buying rights or selling rights, knowing where and how to identify a suitable partner is critical to making product licensing an integral part of your strategy. Literary agents make a business out of doing just that, trying to match a seller with the right buyer. And, as I discuss later in this chapter, you may want to consider working with an agent in some foreign markets. But for the most part, you are likely to find a buyer or seller by personally attending one of the major international book fairs.

Even though we live in an age of instant communication, with ubiquitous e-mail being used 24/7, there is still much to gain from physically getting together with fellow publishers and extolling, in person, the benefits of our respective publications. It is not just a question of nostalgia or some quaint sense of the importance of continuing a long-standing tradition. Rather, books fairs give us the opportunity to meet new people, strengthen existing relationships, get a closer look at new products, and browse in the company of people who are engaged in the same activity and are helping to build the community.

In many cases, during the course of successful projects, you will develop long-term relationships that will be important foundations for future business partnerships. If you have a good relationship with someone in one company, you are likely to maintain that contact and the relationship if he or she moves to another company, assuming, of course, that the new firm also provides a good match for your products, values, and objectives.

Of course, it's possible to develop long-term business relationships without attending book fairs. But these frenetic congresses of like-minded people provide a stimulating atmosphere that allows us to measure our own ideas on a world stage, test our assumptions about what is marketable, and even get lucky by locating, serendipitously, just the right product. Everyone who attends them agrees that being at book fairs is essential to making key contacts and building a competitive publishing program. If book fairs have been able to remain relevant in a world that takes broadband (and increasingly wireless) connectivity for granted in businesses and schools, as well as most households, they are bound to be relevant for quite some time. And if there is little indication that attendance at book fairs is waning, it's because the community wants it that way.

International Town Halls

There are four well-attended international book fairs for the annual exchange of books in all categories of publishing: The Frankfurt Book Fair, which takes place in October; the London Book Fair, which takes place in March; the Bologna Children's Book Fair, which takes place in late March or early April after the London Book Fair; and Book Expo America (BEA, formerly the ABA, or American Bookseller's Association), which takes place in late May and rotates among New York, Chicago, and L.A., with Washington, D.C., added to the rotation in 2006. There are other large book fairs in locations such as Japan, Singapore, India, and China, but these tend to be regional rather than major international events. Certainly the Beijing International Book Fair (BIBF) is gaining in popularity as China becomes more of a world player in international publishing and makes real and visible progress in their respect for and protection of international copyright laws. The BIBF may, in fact, be an essential destination if you are serious about doing meaningful business in China. But the big four—Frankfurt, London, Bologna, and BEA—are the book fairs that most publishers, large and small, attend.

The Frankfurt Book Fair, which has been held continuously at the Frankfurt exhibition complex (known as the *Messe*) since 1949, is the grand-daddy of the fairs. It is by far the biggest, the most talked about, and the one fair that continues to grow year after year. Because the fair attracts so many exhibitors from all over the world, there are very few other venues besides Frankfurt that could easily play host to it. At one point there was talk that the Frankfurt Book Fair might move to

"We can't afford to do sales trips, so we rely on book fairs to meet our customers. There is no alternative to meeting, getting to know, and even making friends with customers. . . . Frankfurt and Bologna are six months apart, perfect for keeping projects on the boil. We are selling rights as well as presenting new titles. We can discover a lot of market information. . . . We can also meet our home market customers 'under one roof.' We could send information by email, but as the market is so competitive, only carefully built-up personal relationships would give us any hope of concluding a sale."

--Catherine Bruzzone Publisher, b small publishing, U.K.

Munich, which also has a large exhibition hall and is, perhaps, a more interesting and hospitable city. In addition, there had been complaints about the inflationary hotel rates in Frankfurt and simply an overall desire for change. After all, Frankfurt is not an especially attractive destination, and in October it can be particularly bleak. But the fair officials recently agreed to put a cap on fee increases, and the hotels in the area have agreed to eliminate the annoying minimum stay requirements and normalize their rates. In exchange, the fair will stay in Frankfurt until at least 2010. Given the tradition behind the fair and the mammoth undertaking in moving a fair of this size, this is a probably a positive outcome for everyone.

Approximately 7,000 exhibitors from more than 100 countries attend the Frankfurt Book Fair each year, and there are hundreds of German publishers on top of that. Publishers are spread out among a complex of a dozen massive buildings, or "halls," which are accessible by minibus or a maze of moving sidewalks and escalators. Hall 8 is where all of the American, British, and international (most others except French, German, and Italian) publishers traditionally exhibit. French and Italian publishers are located in the halls connected to Hall 8, which makes it convenient for browsing through recent publications and design innovation from Europe. German publishers are located in Halls 1 through 4. To avoid the congestion and maddening confusion inside the halls and the connecting corridors, take the mini-buses when moving from hall to hall. Although they can be crowded, they travel continuously and frequently. The halls are well marked on the exterior of the buildings, so the buses, which move freely from building to building, are the easiest way to get around the fair.

Most publishers think about the annual book-fair cycle as beginning with Frankfurt, even though it takes place in the fourth quarter of the calendar year. Big titles (like Bill Clinton's massive autobiography) get their international debut at Frankfurt, and many of the more substantial deals are sealed or announced at the fair. Some of these deals are announced in a daily newsletter that the fair distributes to all exhibitors. For all practical purposes, the new publishing year begins with this fair, and publishers finalize their spring lists at this time.

The London Book Fair (LBF) is the major global spring event for booksellers and is a critical event for the European consumer book trade. In 2006 it moved from Olympia, where it had been for years, to a new venue, ExCel London at the Docklands, in theory to better accommodate the growing number of exhibitors and to make the event more comfortable for browsing. That moved failed to please fairgoers, however, who found the location inconvenient to London hotels and restaurants. So it's moving back to central London to Earls Court One in 2007 for what we hope will be the long term. The LBF is quite a bit smaller than Frankfurt, with less than 1,000 exhibitors, but it's really the best place to discover and learn more about the best book designers and publishers in the English language as well as the U.K. retail market.

The Bologna Children's Book Fair is also worth attending if you have children's and educational products that you want to buy, sell, or license. This fair has always been a favorite among publishers who enjoy the charming medieval architecture of the city, the superb Bolognese cuisine, and the relaxed pace of the fair, especially compared to the frenetic environment that characterizes Frankfurt and, to a somewhat lesser degree, London. The weather is normally better than it is in either Frankfurt or London. It gets roughly the same amount of attendance as the LBF in a far more relaxed atmosphere. With a focus on children's publications, it is inherently less daunting than the other fairs and allows publishers who specialize in children's publications—either trade publications or educational materials—to find one another more easily.

BookExpo America (BEA) is primarily for North American booksellers, distributors, and retailers. Over the years, as the large chains such as Barnes & Noble, Borders, and Books-A-Million—and, of course, Amazon—have dominated the retail trade and fewer independent booksellers have been able to compete, BEA has been expanding its role and its relevancy to include more of the same types of activities that take place at Frankfurt and London. Increasingly, it is an event for the exchange of literary rights, international promotions, big book deals, networking, and celebrity author signings. As the largest book publishing event in the U.S., it's an essential destination for trade publishers and distributors.

These fairs are all considered *international* book fairs because the major international publishers and packagers (people who make books for other publishers and don't actually distribute under their own imprint) attend, and they attract publishers from around the world. For the most part, publishers will send their top executives to these fairs in addition to their foreign rights managers. If you are looking for an international partner in any country, it is more than likely that you will find that partner at one of these events, as well as the right person with whom to work.

Regional Meeting Places

If you publish for a highly specialized market, are looking for a specific type of book from a certain country, or believe that your publication is particularly suited to a specific foreign market, you might want to attend one of the top regional book fairs around the world. Specialty book fairs such as those in Paris, Tokyo, Guadalajara, Singapore, and Jerusalem may be worth attending, depending on your interests. The Beijing Book Fair has been aggressively promoting itself as more than just a regional fair. And certainly given the size and complexity of that market, it's bound to be an increasingly important event. In addition, the Chinese government's recent emphasis on children learning English is making it an important destination for British and American publishers who specialize in developing programs for English as a foreign language (EFL).

If you are primarily interested in interactive, video, and digital content, you might want to consider MIPTV, which takes place in Cannes, France. It used to be called MILIA—when multimedia first hit the publishing stage—and then morphed into an audiovisual marketplace when CD-ROMs and DVD-ROMs started to decline.

Although I have indicated the dates when these fairs take place, they do change from time to time. Frankfurt in October is a tradition and is unlikely to make a calendar move in the near future. But MIPTV, when it was MILIA, used to be in April and is now in October, overlapping a day or two with Frankfurt. You can find the exact dates when these fairs take place, along with a list of past attendees and the areas in which they publish, by visiting the fairs' Web sites. For convenience, I have included a list of the international book fairs by region in Appendix A and useful Web sites in Appendix B at the back of this book.

Preparing for a Fair

Attending one or more of these fairs is really the first step in getting serious about acquiring or selling book rights. Ideally you will want to invest in exhibiting at the fair, so that you have a place to show your books or concepts and to meet people. But many first-timers or small publishers do not rent exhibit space. Instead, they simply "walk the floors" looking for a suitable partner by visiting exhibit booths, browsing the offerings, and hoping to stumble upon just the right property.

An alternative to taking your own space at a fair or to wandering around, lugging your books and "best sellers" behind you in a wheeled Samsonite, is to exhibit with a "collective," which provides a turnkey solution for exhibiting at a minimal cost. Collectives rent and manage a large block of exhibit booths and offer a menu of services including branding, marketing, a place for you to ship products, and a message service so you don't have to send your own staff if you can't afford to. Collectives are available at all of the major fairs, some of which are organized by countries and others by marketing groups or associations. Information on these collectives can also be found at the book fairs' Web sites.

If you are a first-time fairgoer, you should not feel compelled to have a fixed presence at the fair. Plenty of people go without renting real estate just to see how fairs are organized, understand the dynamics, and make initial contacts. There is only so much that you can learn from Web sites or other people's experiences. At some point, you have to find out first-hand whether it's worthwhile to put a physical stake in the ground.

How you approach an international book fair and how much success you can expect to have depends, to some degree, on whether you are buying or selling. More people attend a fair to sell than to buy. Unlike other markets, where supply and demand tends to fluctuate, book fairs always provide a buyer's market. It is far more likely that you will be able to find what you want if you are buying than to sell even your most treasured publications.

There are, however, certain factors that will always favor the seller. For example, it will be relatively easy to find a publisher in, say, Germany, willing to acquire the translation rights to a best seller from a major market such as the U.S. or the U.K. So if you have a best seller on your hands, you are likely to find several bidders for your property. Sought-after brands and trademarks, as well as new publications from well-known publishing houses, do better than those from less known or untested sources. On the other hand, if you publish in a specialty category that has a narrow market or is experiencing a downturn (art history or Middle East travel, respectively), it will be harder to find someone in a foreign market willing to take on the translation rights or even publish the book in English.

When you decide to attend a book fair, it's important to plan ahead by making as many appointments as possible starting three to four months in advance of the fair. Although it's possible to make valuable connections by attending a fair cold and relying on finding a suitable buyer by chance, you will find that most of the people with whom you want to meet will have full schedules. To get on their calendars, you will need to confirm a time as early as possible.

If you don't already have a network of publishers that you can call on, and you are not sure how to find a likely candidate to partner with, you can review the LMP (*Literary Marketplace*), online or in print. The print and electronic versions are available in domestic and international editions; the latter is called the *International Literary Marketplace* (ILMP). You can find it at your local library or simply visit the LMP Web site. This will give you a starting point for locating publishers in other countries that share your interests.

The larger book fairs, such as Frankfurt and Bologna, also put out their own publications of attendees. You might want to review past editions of the fair publications to get a capsule description of the publishers who attended or better yet, go to the book fair Web sites where their catalogue databases are available free of charge. The Frankfurt Book Fair site, for example, has three catalogues online: The main Frankfurt Catalogue, which contains the approximately 7,000 companies that attend; the *Who's Who Catalogue*, which lists around 14,000 publishing and media professionals who attend the fair; and a *Rights Catalogue*, which is a directory of more than 19,000 titles available for subsidiary rights. The online directories make it easy to contact fair attendees to make appointments.

"While English is now the functioning world language, it is a predictable need that either in-house or out-source intermediaries will be required to successfully develop the Chinese market to its fullest potential."

--Tom Murphy
President, Professional Publishing Services

Working with Agents

Although international book fairs are critical to making the right connections, it's not practical—or even desirable—to attend all of them. You might go to two or three, depending on your publishing focus or niche. For this reason, a good way to "keep things moving" overseas while you are home is to have a local agent working on your behalf. You can locate agents at the "rights" sections of the major book fairs, or you might find them at joint country exhibits (the "collectives" mentioned above), which tend to consist of a consortia of publishers, packagers, publishers' representatives, and agents from one country or region. You can also find them listed in the same publications where you will find publishers. The value of agents is that they usually know their market in depth as well as which publishers would be the best fit for your products. Moreover, they can be on site when you can't be. The downside of working with agents, however, is that they don't necessarily know your content as well you expect them to and they usually represent a virtual basketful of products from a variety of publishers. This can be frustrating as you wait for agents to make you and your products their top priority. Once agents do get a nibble, they have a tendency to oversell, over- promise, and try to convince you to accept terms quickly just to get the deal done. In many ways, they can be similar to real estate brokers and favor the quick sale over the right one. Still, in many regions, agents can be a useful part of your overall licensing efforts. They just shouldn't be your primary or only representatives.

When working with agents make sure to pay them only when they conclude a deal. The usual agent commission is 10% of your net royalties, including any advances you receive. When you make a deal with an agent, the agent normally makes the deal with the local publisher directly on your behalf. In this way, the transaction itself goes through the agent first; the local publisher pays the agent, the agent takes his or her cut and passes the balance to you. This actually works well. The agents I've done business with in this way all have been honest and competent in handling these kinds of transactions. What you don't want to do is work with an agent on a retainer basis. This is more often than not a formula for disaster. It generally breeds complacency, and only in rare cases can you count on recovering the fixed investments you made in the agents' fees, travel costs, and other expenses from any deal that they are likely to get for you. The best formula is to pay only for results. Most good agents will expect to work in this way.

Although there is nothing wrong with an agent acting on your behalf during a large part of the negotiations—even as the project moves into the development or production phase—you should make sure that there is a way for you to establish a personal relationship with the publisher. Agents may come and go, but you and your partner need to be confident that there is more that binds you than an agent, including a good working relationship and common goals. Even if for expediency, or any other reason, the project has to begin prior to your meeting the publisher, you should plan on meeting face to face at some point—if not at the publisher's place of business, then at least at one of the international book fairs.

Try This!

Use book fairs as a place to form relationships and make friends in addition to finding specific properties. Strong industry relationships will put you on the fast track for new products before publishers release them. In addition, good relationships will make it easier to sell rights. Building trust with your potential partners should be your primary objective.

Chapter 5

Strategies for Buying and Selling Rights

Broken down into their primary economic units, books and publications in any format—print or electronic—are known collectively as intellectual property. The buying and selling of intellectual property rights, or licensing, is the basis of co-publishing deals. As a seller of intellectual property, your goal is to partner with like-minded publishers who have the ability to maximize the potential of your products in their markets. If you are fortunate enough to have a particularly desirable property, you may have more than one potential partner and may be able to get several people to bid on your property. However, this is not the norm. Except for best sellers or publications by well-known authors, it's not easy to find a willing and effective co-publishing partner.

That's why everyone loves a buyer. If you are looking to acquire a book, or a series of books, either outright or for the purposes of translating or adapting them for your market, you will have a relatively easy time making appointments at a book fair. The main reason why people exhibit at fairs is to promote and sell their products; everyone will be eager to tell you about the merits of their products in the hopes of convincing you to make a commitment—on the spot, if possible. Assuming that you and your partner can agree on the general terms of the deal, it's generally first come, first served. Unless the property has already established itself as a best seller, publishers won't wait to get competitive bids. In the business of licensing, the rule of thumb is a bird in the hand.

Getting Started

If you are a potential buyer and are shopping around for product, you have to be extremely focused to make sure that you spend time with people who really have what you want. Publishers and packagers, in general, can only sell you what they have, and that may not be exactly what you are looking for. Or they will take a lot of time fishing through their backlists trying to find some hope of life out of a dated product.

Ideally what book packagers prefer to do is to license the same product in as many languages as possible, control all aspects of the project including the manufacturing, combine the various versions to get the unit quantities as high as possible, and print all the versions at the same time—thereby reducing the manufacturing costs and increasing their margins. This is a typical co-publishing scenario. Although the more versions that the packager can produce at the same time the greater its profit, the co-publishers also benefit from the cost savings due to the higher print runs and resulting lower unit costs.

Some book packagers will be willing to customize a project for you or even build a product from scratch according to your specifications. But this is a much more expensive way to acquire a product and doesn't take advantage of the economies of co-publishing. Be sure to be as specific as you can when discussing your needs, and be sure to make appointments only with partners that match your profile.

As a publisher, when you set out to create a product, you most likely did enough research to determine that there was a market for it that you could reach with your available resources and through your normal channels of distribution. You also determined the right amount of investment to make in order to turn a profit over an acceptable period of time. However, unless you have had a lot of international experience or have company-owned overseas operations, you probably didn't build into your business model incremental revenue from licensing deals in foreign markets.

If you are a seller, the goal of licensing a product to someone in another country is to take advantage of markets that you can't easily reach through your established distribution channels. This will generate licensing revenue, which is an excellent way to earn incremental income from your investment in a product without incurring the costs of sales and marketing in other countries. The assumption is that, on your own, you have neither the means nor the expertise to sell your product in the foreign market. By licensing your product to a publisher in another market, you shift the burden of adapting, translating (if necessary), producing, marketing, and selling your product to the licensee. This is usually a win-win. Your partner, the licensee, takes advantage of the investments you made in conceiving, writing, and developing the product; and you, the licensor, will benefit from your partner's understanding of, and ability to serve, a particular

"We sold our first bilingual English-Spanish series for very young children to Barron's in the U.S.A. about 15 years ago and since then they have reprinted regularly and also bought other series of bilingual books from us which they reprint regularly. It is a steady relationship: their buyers have remained the same and we have continued to produce books they find successful."

--Catherine Bruzzone Publisher, b small publishing, U.K.

market. The revenue you get from this, in the form of royalties, goes right to your bottom line.

The Elements of a Deal

Is there a typical or standard licensing deal? The answer is not really, but there are some basic parameters that everyone follows. Of course, how you approach the deal depends on whether you are buying or selling. (Just as the joke goes about the rug merchant who asks his son how much two plus two is, and the son replies, "Am I buying or selling?") If you are buying, your goal will be to pay as little as possible and "even less" if you have to incur translating expenses. If you are selling, your goal is to get as much as possible, including a substantial advance payment and a meaningful minimal annual commitment. These are the starting positions from each perspective. But the goal for both sides, in any negotiation, is to make sure that it works two ways. Both parties need to generate enough revenue to make the transaction worthwhile. The long-term goal is to establish a valuable relationship that creates a trustworthy basis for conducting many fruitful transactions.

Any deal should be market driven. So if you are selling, you will want your potential partner to identify, quantitatively, what the sales potential is for your product in his market. He should be able to forecast how many units he can sell in a typical 12-month period and at what price. Presumably, these are data points that he knows better than you do in his territory and, as result, should provide a basis for going forward. If he's the right partner, his estimates will be fairly accurate—at least within a reliable range. Of course, there is always some risk in launching any new product; an experienced publisher knows how to weigh the risks against the opportunities. And by licensing a product, rather than developing one from scratch, the risks to your partner are dramatically reduced.

Your partner represents a new "territory" to you. Normally a territory is defined by language rather than physical boundaries. Publishers licensing French-language rights, for example, would normally include Switzerland and Belgium in their territory, but it's important to spell out the territory precisely. French-language rights could also include Quebec and far-flung French territories such as Mauritius. Identifying as many appropriate territories as possible from the beginning will benefit both sides. Neither of you should make assumptions about what territories are "automatically" included. This should not be left open for debate after the marketing and selling begins.

If you are an American publisher, you will normally define your territory as the U.S. and Canada, but be sure to specify U.S.-owned territories as well, such as Puerto Rico and Guam, if you are able to reach them effectively. Don't assume that these territories just "come with the territory." In any case, it's important to make sure that you and your partner understand where in the world the licensing rights apply.

In addition to territory or markets, the basic elements of any deal are the following:

✧ Periodic royalties;

✧ Advances against future royalties;

✧ Minimum guarantees; and

✧ A defined term limit.

Any deal should address these elements. Royalties may be at a fixed rate, or they could increase or even decrease over time. Advances can be paid up front or periodically—every year, for example. However, minimum guarantees are not always a given. There may be reasons, which I discuss later, to either insist on them or forego them.

The deal should be structured so that you, as the licensor, receive a royalty stream based on your partner's net receipts, which generally means the revenue kept after deducting the cost of goods and factors in any discounts and sales expenses. You need to make sure that you both define "net receipts" in the same way. Some people will deduct development costs or marketing expenses before calculating net receipts. This is always a point of discussion and negotiation.

Royalty rates vary, but the range is typically between 5 and 15 percent, depending on development costs and any ongoing third party expenses that might provide additional financial burdens on the publisher. Royalties can be calculated quarterly or twice a year, and generally, they are paid along with the submission of an accounting report on specific dates.

Royalties are not always calculated on net receipts. Some publishers prefer to base them on the selling price of the book or, in some cases, as a fixed dollar amount. I've always thought that net receipts, when defined correctly, is fair for everyone and gives the publisher the flexibility needed to offer discounts or to make bulk deals without worrying about possibly losing money or drastically reducing margins because of fixed royalty commitments. If a publisher doesn't have the flexibility to maximize all marketing opportunities, neither the publisher nor the royalty earner will benefit in the long term. The publisher may simply have to turn down business because royalty obligations make it financially unviable. That scenario must be avoided and can be easily by defining net receipts in a way that allows the publisher the ability to take advantage of opportunities that may not be anticipated at the time that the agreement is made.

Once you agree on the royalty rate and how it is going to be calculated, you need to establish an acceptable advance payment that will be applied against future royalties. Advances are important because they help determine your partner's seriousness. The more that a company invests up front in the product, the more likely that it will get the product to market quickly and put together a meaningful marketing campaign. Any advances, however, should not be too onerous and should take into consideration the investment that your partner has to make to accommodate its market's expectations, including, of course, the cost of translation. In the end, advances should be in line with anticipated earnings. If, for example, you have both agreed to quarterly royalty payments, a typical royalty advance should be equal to the royalties that you expect to earn from the first quarter's forecasted revenues.

I need to clarify that the kinds of publications that these benchmarks apply to are educational titles, general reference works, travel books, and most children's books. When it comes to blockbusters, celebrity books, best sellers, or "star" titles with unusual marketing hype or potential, other standards are likely to apply. Although the royalty rates may be similar, advances may be very substantial and even speculative. In these elite publishing categories where there is often a lot of competitive bidding for the original publication as well as foreign-language and even movie rights, advances can reach six and even seven figures. In some cases, these advances may not be recoverable over the lifespan of the book, and publishers can end up incurring huge losses on the publication when sales fail to meet the astronomical expectations driven by the advances. A good place to follow the trends in royalty advances with these types of books is in *PublishersLunch*, an online newsletter that you can subscribe to for free, or *The Book Standard*, also available only online.

Advances are normally paid out over time: a percentage upon signing the contract, another portion at some stage during production, and a final payment due when the product goes to press. None of this is set in stone, but if you use these parameters as a starting point, you will be following standard industry practices.

In addition to royalties and advances against future royalties, you need to consider the two other basic factors before finalizing the deal: the term, or length of time, of the contract and minimum guarantees.

Term limits are typical in any licensing agreement. Three- or five-year limits are standard. Sometimes minimum guarantees are established during the initial term of the agreement and sometimes they are not. You might, however, base the length of time that you are willing to give up rights in a market on set minimum guarantees. In other words, the term limit could be extended provided that defined revenue hurdles have been reached. In this way, your partner can continue to publish a product that is finding success in its market—obviously building momentum—and you benefit from the positive results. There is no need to terminate an agreement as long as both parties are benefiting from the relationship.

It is not easy to get people to agree to minimums, so if you press for them, the amounts must be realistic. Unfortunately, there are a certain number of unknowns in publishing, and how a specific market will actually respond to a new product is the most vexing one of all. Determining what is realistic is more of an art than a science. What you want to avoid is a situation where your minimum guarantees are unnecessarily high and actually **exceed** the amount of the earned royalties. This may sound like a good deal for the licensor, but it's likely to be a short-lived benefit. In this scenario, it is unlikely that the licensee will be motivated to renew the license at the end of the term, ending a revenue stream for the licensor and putting the licensor in the position of having to start all over. Far more preferential is the situation where earned royalties are in excess of the minimum guarantees. This means that the product is exceeding expectations, which is a far better result for both parties. If this is the case, both parties will be eager to continue the relationship beyond the initial term.

The nature of licensing assumes that the licensor and the licensee each have their mutually beneficial roles in a relationship. There is an acknowledgment on the part of the licensee that the intellectual property holder took a risk in developing a product in the first place and invested a significant amount of resources in bringing the product to market. The licensee is able to take advantage of this "vision" and head start. At the same time, the licensor must be able to assume that the licensee will make the incremental investment necessary to bring the product into a specific market and, in so doing, will return revenues from a market that was previously inaccessible to the licensor.

The process of establishing minimums and reporting earned royalties assumes, of course, that the accounting will be trustworthy. Some publishers will insist on certain minimums because they feel that they cannot trust the licensee's royalty reports and, therefore, will count on the minimums to make the deal worth pursuing. They will set the minimums high enough so that they do not have to worry about the accuracy of the royalty reports. This is a strategy, but it's not a good basis for building trust or long-term relationships. You should approach a deal like this only if there is no better alternative.

Another way to license a product without the burden of calculating royalties or establishing minimum guarantees is to buy finished goods on a royalty-inclusive basis. In this way, you are actually purchasing product (paying for manufactured goods) but with the same rights that you would be granted from a straight licensing deal. In other words, you are buying the intellectual property rights **and** the physical product itself. This is a basic turnkey deal. The originating publisher or packager will construct a deal on finished books for a set unit fee—and also take a small margin on the manufacturing. The fee will be "fully loaded," meaning that the royalty is already built into the cost of goods.

This is a very simple way for everyone to calculate their risks and to keep the post-publication accounting issues at a minimum. It also simplifies the entire process for the licensee, who doesn't have to do any development work. It's also a common way for a co-publishing developer with several licensing deals going at the same time will also frequently work this way. As I indicated earlier in the chapter, the developer will print several language

"Our business is focused on books as well as our know-how, but we keep a sharp eye on all the other media and look for partners in different categories. We need print projects that can have multimedia extensions."

--Hans-Peter Gutmann
Gutmann+Gutmann,
Germany

versions at once to take advantage of printing economies.

But there are downsides to this type of deal. The amount of adaptation that the licensee can make is limited since the structure or layout and design of the content is predetermined. In addition, as the buyer, you have to commit to a substantial print run up front in order to secure a favorable unit price point. Usually these print runs are higher than you would normally contract for if you controlled the production and manufacturing yourself.

Asset Acquisition

Licensing content or developing it yourself are not the only ways to build your list. Content can also be bought and sold outright, just as companies are acquired, either in whole or by business units. There are times when you might want to consider acquiring content, either in the form of publication lists or random assets, instead of building it from scratch or licensing it. And the fact that so much content is now available in a digital format makes it easier than ever to evaluate content, even from remote sources, to determine whether it makes sense to acquire.

At any given time, there may be a number of companies that are looking to divest themselves of assets that, for one reason or another, no longer fit into their strategic plan or corporate profile. There may be nothing wrong with these properties, but for a variety of reasons the company's management has decided that it makes more sense to sell them than to either continue to maintain and market them or manage the in-house licensing process.

Many smaller companies have been built on making acquisitions of this type. Other companies have been able to grow or to expand into new markets by acquiring product lines in this way. If you have available capital and are looking to grow, or if you are in a mature market segment and need to make a move into a higher growth sector, you should consider looking at potential acquisition targets.

There are several ways to search for good acquisitions. Book fairs are unlikely to be the best place since the focus at those events is on buying and selling individual properties rather than entire companies, divisions, or product lines. Instead, you should network with investment banks that specialize in brokering intellectual property or are purchasing media companies for their own portfolios, which is becoming increasingly common. You might want to contact various publishing associations, such as the Association of Educational Publishers (AEP), The Association of American Publishers (AAP), or the Software & Information Industry Association (SIIA) to help you locate investment banks that may provide the best fit for your interests. The private equity firms that specialize in the publishing sector, such as Berkery, Noyes & Co. or Veronis Suhler Stevenson, are often affiliate members of these associations and sponsor various networking events. You should also check industry publications such as *Publisher's Weekly* or *The Book Standard* and begin to follow the trends to learn about who is buying whom and what companies or product lines may be up for sale. But in order to get a jump on the process and to enter the picture at the early stages, you want to be on the brokers' A-list.

Wrapping Things Up

The purpose of this chapter was to provide strategies for buying and selling rights that are grounded in the basic economies of general publishing and what both sides are able to bring to the table. As the originator of a product, the licensor has not only taken on the initial risks of the project, but has

"The biggest changes in the marketplace are with the distribution channels. I look for the right ways of distribution for any publishing product— the right way may be different from country to country and it may not be the classic bookstore channel."

--Sebastian Gutmann
Gutmann+Gutmann,
Germany

invested time and resources that the licensee does not have to invest. Even if the licensee now has to translate and perhaps even reconfigure the product, the original IP holder has decreased the licensee's time to market and has provided a fully developed concept.

It is my view that the origination of the product entitles the licensor to own any derivatives of the product, including translations and additional content regardless of the format. In other words, if you are the licensor and are licensing a product that will be translated and adapted, you should retain the rights to the translation. Any work that the licensee does is based on the licensor's original work and is "fruit of the same tree." The licensee can have the rights to the translation as long as the contract is active, but once the contract has terminated, all rights, including the translated materials, should revert to the licensor.

At the same time, if the licensor feels that there is value in the licensee's adaptation, the agreement made between the two parties should allow the licensor to use in its respective market any or all of the licensee's derivative work.

From a seller's point of view, licensing products into a new territory that you cannot reach is an excellent way to extend the earning power of a product in which you have already made a substantial investment. Publishing has a high fixed, but low variable, cost. Licensing is the optimal "variable," because the revenue it generates is purely incremental. From a buyer's, or licensee's, point of view, licensing a product is an excellent way to take advantage of someone else's capital risk in development. In other words, when compared to the publisher's original investment in research, development, and production, the licensee's additional costs to make the market appropriate are minimal; at least they should be. And since royalties are paid only after working off initial advances and after actual sales are made, royalty expenses do not negatively impact cash flow.

You may eventually get to the point where you cringe at making high royalty payments, but you have to keep in mind the much smaller risk you took in the first place. If you are sending large royalty checks, it means that your bet on the original property is paying off. So, in reality, the higher the royalty checks are, the happier you should be.

Try This!

Focus on the long-term value of your relationships. You should be developing relationships, not transactions. Think of everything you ask for and everything you agree to as a step toward building long-lasting relationships. Don't let contract details, such as royalty percentages or advances, interfere with the ultimate goal.

Chapter 6

Rights and Wrongs—The Basis of a *Good* Deal

When you are establishing the basis on which you are going to sell one of your properties, it's important to have realistic expectations. You could very easily come to the wrong conclusions based on incorrect assumptions about the size of a market or the kind of barriers that a distributor in that market may face. For example, you may assume that since India has a population of almost one billion people, the market for your product should be three times what it would be in North America. But since the earning power per capita in India is extremely small compared to that of the U.S. and Canada, you will need to manage down your expectations proportionately. All markets are price sensitive, but in order to understand what this means in places like India and South America, price sensitivity has to be viewed from inside the market—not from a North American or European perspective.

"The most difficult legal issue is getting enough money up front to make the deal worthwhile, since some overseas companies don't give you royalty reports you can believe, or payments."

--*Dave Oliphant*
President, OK, Inc.

You will have to make many adjustments to accommodate emerging markets, especially in regard to pricing and methods of distribution. In some markets, such as China, Thailand, and India, you may also have to factor in the risks of piracy or the need to sample products well in advance of a selling cycle. And whatever obstacles don't jump out at you immediately, your potential partner should call to your attention. When you end up factoring in the "obvious" things that could possibly affect your opportunities in certain markets and take into consideration that you may end up with some unpleasant surprises, almost any deal you can make that gives you some fixed revenue up front may be better than any potential upsides based on royalties.

Even though China and Thailand, for example, may require special consideration, with more inherent obstacles than, say, European markets, the basic issues are applicable almost anywhere. Every market will have its unique set of factors that will affect the marketability of a product, so your goal should be to establish a relationship with the best possible partner. A good partner will help you navigate the vagaries of the market and will be able to avoid pitfalls that you could not anticipate. In the end, a relationship that can eliminate or at least dramatically reduce the problems that are unique to a specific market is more important than the specific terms of any written agreement.

The Value of Setting Limits

In the previous chapter, I indicated that every licensing agreement should have a term limit. This is central to safeguarding your original investment and in putting the burden on your partner to maximize the value of your product. If you are both happy with the market penetration and financial performance of the product at the end of the term, there is no reason why the agreement can't be renewed or extended for an additional length of time. On the other hand, if you are not happy with the arrangement at the end of the initial term, you will have the opportunity to move the product somewhere else.

One extremely important aspect of a term limit, and part of the formula for making sure you have constructed a good deal, is not to allow the term of the agreement to renew automatically unless the specified minimum guarantees are achieved or a new term limit is established. The term of the agreement should be allowed to expire, and the license should not renew unless someone takes definitive action to renew it and both parties agree to the new terms. An expiration date gives both parties an opportunity to re-examine the relationship and quantify the viability of the product for both sides. In addition, it prevents the unhappy situation where the people who originally concluded the deal have since departed from the company and have left others with an open-ended, perpetual agreement that they can't undo. Since I have faced this situation myself, I make sure that I don't put others in this position. No one should be in a position to live with something that contractually can't be undone. There are always ways to get out of a bad situation, but by establishing a fixed expiration date, you provide the maximum amount of flexibility for everyone.

The purpose of minimum guarantees and their function in a good deal is to help motivate performance and to provide an incentive on the part of the licensee to exert best efforts. Minimum guarantees are harder to negotiate and involve much more risk on the part of the licensee, but the subject should be raised as part of any good negotiation. Sometimes you can have minimums that escalate over time, so that you give your partner an opportunity to build market momentum and recover initial investments in launching the product. Ongoing product investments will naturally decrease over time, which will then allow for greater guarantees as the product

"We find that the pattern of buying in foreign markets goes up and down. One year activity books are all the rage in one market; the next year that market isn't buying any activity books. We have to try to maintain relationships with everyone even if they don't buy for a number of years and at the same time find new customers. Central Europe and Japan are two markets we have not yet cracked."

--Catherine Bruzzone Publisher, b small publishing, U.K

matures and gains traction in the market.

Whether you have established minimums, or even hold your partner accountable for agreed-upon minimums, you should always have some expectations in mind that will cause you either to renew or terminate the agreement at the end of the established term limit. If you do have minimum guarantees built into the agreement, you and your partner will go through a learning curve to determine whether the minimums were appropriate or not; and sometimes failing to achieve these minimums may not be anyone's fault. Before you pull the plug on a partner for not meeting minimums, especially a partner who operates in good faith, make sure that you really understand that market, that you have evidence that your product is being undersold, and that you believe that your product is better off in someone else's hands. Don't change partners without a good reason. It's much easier to fix a product problem or a poor marketing plan than to develop a new mutually beneficial relationship.

Establishing Realistic Targets

Advances against future royalties are generally the norm, but they aren't an absolute requirement. Further, there is no standard amount or fixed ratio against a forecast. Usually, this is a good-faith number and a token expression of commitment. Sometimes, however, especially in a competitive situation, an advance can well exceed any definition of "token" and can be a serious commitment that may be difficult to recover. As was discussed in the previous chapter, it's common to make the advance equivalent to what you believe the first quarter's royalties will be—based on the royalty rate, price points, and sales forecasts. That may or may not be appropriate. If your partner has to invest significant resources in translating or adapting the product, the amount of the advance should take that factor into consideration. In the long run, you should be more interested in the long-term value of the product in the market, not in the instant gratification of an advance.

Another way to motivate a licensee to perform without creating an unnecessary burden is to make sure that the agreement specifies a target date for publication. Or, to achieve the same end, you can make the first royalty payment due by a certain date after signing the agreement. Either way, you need to make sure that the licensee really intends to publish your work and is not just holding onto the rights in order to prevent someone else from publishing it. This doesn't happen very often, but it can, depending on the market and the competitive climate. On the other hand, the licensee may have had all intentions of publishing the product but simply ran out of funds or had a change in priorities. Regardless of the intentions or reasons for missing a publication date, the result, as far as you are concerned, is the same. You can't receive revenue if the licensee does not publish the product with a solid marketing plan in place. Unless there are commitments built into the contract with specific time requirements, there would be no urgency for the licensee to publish by a specific date.

Make sure that you buy or sell only those rights that are likely to be used. For example, your partner may intend on publishing the product only in print form. If this is the case, there is no reason to include electronic rights in the deal. As we discussed earlier, territory can be another issue to consider. A publisher in France may ask for the rights for the entire French-speaking world, which is absolutely fine and logical if it has the resources and distribution network to market in all of the places that would be considered part of this territory. Quebec and Mauritius, for example, are both French-speaking territories on opposite sides of the globe. Does your France-based partner get to these distant locations? If not, you might want to specify which French-speaking markets can realistically be reached and assign rights only for those places.

A good rule of thumb is not to seek or grant rights that are not going to be exploited, and don't give away rights that you don't have to. At the same time, make sure that you are not so restrictive in either acquiring or assigning rights that you close out future opportunities.

The idea is to sell as many finished goods or services as possible in as many markets as possible, either by yourself or with your partner. The world is a big marketplace and very few products, as a matter of practice, get a wide enough circulation to worry too much about whose territory is whose. In most cases, it's unlikely that channel conflict is more than a perceived issue.

Wrapping Things Up

The best way to ensure that you have a good deal is to have confidence in your partner. If it's a new relationship, be sure to check his credentials and talk to other publishers who have a track record with the company. At the same time, don't assume that your best bet is with a well-known publisher. In fact, it may not be. You want to find the best fit for your particular publication, and that might require a smaller, more focused publisher who understands your particular market niche.

Make sure that whomever you sell your product to will treat your property just like you would treat it—like it's theirs. You want your partner to take ownership of the product and to give the same kind of editorial and production values, as well as marketing attention, to it that they would their own publications.

Similarly, when you license a product, you should plan on behaving in the same fashion—as if it's one of your babies. If you don't like the deal, if you don't have confidence in the product and its potential, for whatever reason, walk away. It is better that you don't make a deal at all than to end up in a deal that you later regret.

Try This!

If you are not sure that you can take advantage of certain marketing rights, don't insist on them. Similarly, if a potential partner can't take advantage of all channels in all media, don't give everything away. Limit rights to those channels and markets that you know that your partner can exploit and take any others off the table. There is no reason to give up rights that you don't have to.

Chapter 7

Legal Matters

The process for formalizing a workable licensing or co-publishing arrangement consists of having three documents in place:

✧ A mutual non-disclosure (NDA) agreement

✧ A term sheet

✧ A binding agreement or contract

Mutual Non-Disclosure

Regardless of the nature of the deal and how sensitive the negotiations are, it's always prudent to sign a mutual non-disclosure (NDA) or confidentiality agreement. An NDA is meant to be an interim document that can serve as the first step to executing a binding agreement. An NDA will permit you and your partner to exchange information freely, including any information that you might consider to be proprietary or that you expect to be kept confidential. Although an NDA is more common and essential in software licensing where exchanging code can present real business risks to the developer if the code were to be made public, it's a good idea to have a written statement for any exchange of intellectual property that establishes what is at stake and what underlies the confidentiality of the relationship.

The NDA must be mutual, which means that both parties are equally responsible for maintaining the confidentiality of the arrangement and for securing all documents and correspondence that is exchanged. The NDA should require both parties to destroy any documentation related to the other party's intellectual property or the nature of the relationship in the event that they could not come to an agreement. An NDA should have a term limit of between two and five years regardless of whether the deal goes forward or falls apart for some reason.

Starting with a Term Sheet

Assuming you have determined that you are going to proceed with a deal, you and your partner should first exchange a concise list of terms and conditions, a term sheet, that describes the basic elements of the deal, what the mutual obligations are, and what both parties expect a successful outcome to be. This can be as simple as a bulleted list or outline of your intentions, mutual responsibilities, what resources will be employed, and the anticipated mutual financial commitments. The primary purpose of the term sheet is to flush out any issues or areas of disagreement that need to be resolved prior to formalizing an agreement and to get a sound, mutual understanding in place before you make the relationship official. Often it's easier to "see" what the structure of a relationship is in a term sheet, free from the density that is invariably part of any legal document. This should not be a complex document; it should be a basic description in plain language of what each party is willing to commit to.

Using an agreed-upon term sheet as a starting point, you can proceed to formalize the relationship and make it legal by agreeing to terms and conditions in a binding licensing agreement or contract. If you don't have a legal department or even a standard licensing agreement on hand, you don't have to rush out immediately and hire an attorney to have one produced for you. Chances are your partner will have one that will be perfectly acceptable. However, before you sign anything, especially someone else's standard form, you should make sure that it not only accurately represents your business goals as well as the spirit of the term sheet, but that it protects your corporate legal interests.

A Standard Agreement

Most overseas publishers who rely upon licensing or co-publishing as a basic part of their business have a standard agreement—in English—that should serve both of your purposes well. The same is true of publishers who on a regular basis license content **from** other publishers. Again, after the terms and conditions are agreed upon, it's essential to review the document with an intellectual property attorney, but there is no reason why you can't start out with your partner's boilerplate contract.

In the course of doing several agreements, you will eventually be able to piece together an agreement that will suit most of your licensing purposes. Over time, you will likely need to refine and revise it as you gain more experience or as new situations demand. But I don't know of any publisher

"Legally, the biggest issue is the clarity of rights and ownership on termination."

--Ian Grant
Managing Director,
Britannica, U.K.

who is particularly possessive about the agreement itself or the specific language of the agreement. If you like the way a certain agreement is written, and it seems to meet your needs and cover your general business goals, ask the publisher if you can adapt it and use it for your own licensing deals. Most publishers will be happy to make it available. After all, it's likely that they originally borrowed portions of it, if not all of it, from someone else's forms.

Licensing agreements normally consist of four parts:

✧ **Definitions** of terms, conditions, warranties, and other legal covenants that are described in the agreement;

✧ The **terms and conditions** of the business transaction itself, or what you and your partner are agreeing to buy or sell from each other;

✧ The **legal parameters** that attempt to deal with the relationship if or when things go wrong—the kinds of things for which companies end up needing a lawyer; and

✧ The **specifications** of the intellectual property that is being licensed as well as the format in which the content will be transferred.

If you are using a third party's agreement, you will need to have a good IP attorney review at least the legal covenants of the agreement to make sure that you understand what is at risk and what you are committing to and to explain legal terminology or warranties—especially in the case of any disputes—with which you may not be familiar. Even though most standard licensing agreements that I've seen contain a minimum amount of legal jargon, some technical or specifically legal terminology is unavoidable.

If the licensing agreement also allows for the transfer of code or if it includes ongoing software or Web services, make sure you have someone from your IT staff review the agreement as well.

I've included a typical licensing agreement in Appendix C at the back of this book, which is a standard form I have used successfully in several situations. However, to reinforce the point, this is only a sample agreement, and even though it has worked for me, you shouldn't consider it a legal document worth using, let alone signing, until you have an IP attorney approve it.

You, and not your attorney, should assume responsibility for justifying and explaining the basis of the transaction. Articulating the terms and conditions of any agreement is a business function, not a legal one. Your attorney can help structure the language so that it reflects your intentions, protects your IP, and ensures that the deal is consistent with any other legal commitments that you or others in your company may have made. In other words, one of the purposes of a good agreement is to make sure that it does not conflict with other agreements that you have in place. But you shouldn't leave the structuring of the terms and conditions themselves up to your lawyer. You might end up with language that is inconsistent with your intent, or you could over-engineer the deal to the degree that it actually prevents you from complying with the terms. The simpler the agreement, the better it is, and any experienced IP attorney will tell you so.

Since licensing agreements are usually between companies that operate in different countries, there are often three common points of contention:

✧ Which country's laws govern the agreement?

✧ In which country are legal disputes to be resolved?

✧ In what currency will payments be made?

Usually, whoever is marketing the licensed property will expect the agreement to be governed by the laws in his country and to have any legal disputes that may arise resolved there as well. In addition, the licensee, in this case, will probably prefer to make payments in his local currency to avoid taking any risks with exchange-rate fluctuations.

One way to get around the venue problem, or determining whose laws to adopt and where disputes will be resolved, is to apply the laws of a neutral country, such as Switzerland, and to choose a location that is equally difficult to get to by both parties. This is not only fair, but it helps to keep the resolution of problems where they belong—out of the courts and between the two parties.

As far as the currency to be used, you will find that most people will agree to make payments in U.S. dollars if the contract also ensures that they won't be penalized by an unfavorable foreign-exchange rate. Naturally overseas publishers will record their royalty obligations in their local currency and then convert the total amounts to U.S. dollars prior to making payments. Often the conversion rate is written into the agreement. If it is, it shouldn't be fixed for the entire term of the agreement. The contract should make clear that the conversion rate should be reviewed at least quarterly and adjusted, if necessary, against the current prevailing rate. You'll have to agree on a fluctuation range that will be acceptable to both of you.

A Case in Point

I once ran into an issue regarding what currency to use with a Canadian publisher from whom we licensed a series of interactive learning materials. Her concern was legitimate because of the wide fluctuations in the value of the Canadian dollar against the U.S. dollar. She had a small company, and she didn't want to lose critical margins because of an unfavorable exchange rate.

Here's how we resolved this problem. Instead of assigning a royalty against total revenue of sales of the materials, we established a fixed payment for units sold in Canadian dollars regardless of what the exchange rate was. We dealt with the exchange rate issue on our side and paid in U.S. dollars, but the unit value in Canadian dollars was always the same. In this way, our partner knew exactly what she was earning, in her currency, based on the number of units sold.

"The important clauses in our contracts are: a) the length of license; b) the territories; c) the payment terms."

--*Catherine Bruzzone Publisher, b small publishing, U.K.*

Wrapping Things Up

Although the following is not meant to be an exhaustive list, these are the standard terms and conditions that must be part of any licensing agreement. This list summarizes, at a high level, the main points more technically rendered in the sample agreement in Appendix C.

✧ Identification and place of business of the parties entering into the agreement, as well as where the parties are incorporated if different from the place of business

✧ A clear description of the intellectual property

✧ The grant of rights or what the owner of the intellectual property is interested in giving to the licensee (this usually requires detailed elaboration in an appendix)

✧ Specific rights that are being withheld

✧ The territory or places where the licensed property can be sold and any re-licensing rights

✧ Warranties indicating that the licensor owns the property in question and has the right to enter into a licensing agreement, as well as any restrictions or encumbrances that may apply

✧ The term of the agreement—how long the licensee will have rights in his territory—and what performance hurdles will be required in order to extend those rights

✧ The quantity and price agreed to if the licensee is buying finished goods

✧ Deliverables required, such as electronic files, transcripts, or original art, if the licensee is handling production and manufacturing

✧ Terms of payment, specifying royalty rates and any advance against those royalties as well as minimum guarantees

✧ Copyright and trademark notices, including specific language that both parties require

✧ A final publication date

✧ Notice of the reversion of rights back to the licensor when the term of the agreement expires or if the publication date isn't met

✧ The state's or country's laws that govern the agreement and where any arbitration will take place in the event of a dispute

✧ What constitutes a breech of the agreement and what the remedies are in the case of a breech

In addition to the above, the contract must allow for worse-case scenarios, for example, in the case of copyright or trademark infringements, bankruptcies, acts of war and God, and other dire events. These rarely come up in licensing deals, but they must be considered—companies can and do go bankrupt, companies can be bought and sold soon after a deal is signed, and books can sometimes literally be lost at sea. Most boilerplate agreements will have these clauses well articulated; your attorney will make sure that they are there and that they are either slanted in your favor or, at the very least, apply equally and fairly to both parties. At the end of the day, the best agreement is one that enables both parties to achieve their goals, sets the stage for additional deals, and provides the basis of a true relationship and not just a terminal transaction.

Try This!

Make sure that your legal team is involved as early as possible in a project. By using an NDA and a term sheet, you are able to inform legal from the beginning of the project of the basic intentions of both parties. Ultimately, the business people must be responsible for the mechanics of the deal as well as the mutual obligations.

Chapter 8

Avoiding the Blame Game

Ｉf you believe that you have found a partner to work with in a new market, you should verify that he has four key attributes:

✦ Financial stability;

✦ The ability to keep sensitive information, including the nature of your agreement, confidential;

✦ The technology necessary to keep intellectual property secure; and

✦ Excellent communication skills and processes.

All of these are critical qualities for mitigating risk and building the foundation for a strong relationship—and the burden must be shared by both sides. But perhaps the most difficult of all of these to measure and to sustain over the course of a project is communication. I've always believed that it's impossible to over-communicate, even among co-workers that you see and meet with every day in your own office. So it's not hard to imagine that communicating with overseas partners—mostly with e-mails or even frequent videoconferencing—is exponentially more difficult. Learning how to communicate takes a lot of work, experience, skill, patience, and compromise. Its importance in a successful relationship should not be underestimated, and it needs to be continually stressed with your team as well. Otherwise, you will waste a lot of time and money and put the project and long-term relationship at risk.

As the relationship progresses from the contract to the development stage, you should make sure that your best communicators are involved in the project. If necessary, you may have to provide training for your staff to build communication skills among all of the individuals involved in working with any of your overseas projects and partners. It's important that they do not make assumptions and continually validate what they believe is being communicated and agreed to. The validation process, though continuous, needs to be conducted in short intervals.

Once you have identified that a partner has the attributes necessary to be a good partner, you will need to define, as clearly as possible, each other's roles and responsibilities to make sure that you both get the results you want. To a large degree, this will be outlined in the contract, which specifies ownership of the licensed intellectual property as well as any additional material that is developed to bring the product to market; defines the intentions of both parties and delineates mutual obligations; and outlines payment terms, deadlines, and other critical business issues. But the contract cannot cover all of the processes and procedures that must be put into place for the relationship to be successful. Nor can it account for all contingencies or the various issues that may arise in order to get the product to market and maintain a successful relationship. The contract can specify what you intend to do, what the basic deliverables are, and what the costs or fees will be. It doesn't adequately cover, though, how you are going to get things done, and what the options are if things don't go as planned.

After the contract has been executed—by top management or the head of licensing—the individuals who are actually responsible for making the relationship successful, as well as implementing the tasks necessary to complete the project, rarely refer back to the contract itself. In fact, it is possible that they had little or no input in writing or negotiating the terms and conditions of the contract in the first place, even though they may be responsible for the success of the project.

Therefore, a good working relationship between the licensor and licensee will not depend entirely on what is written in the contract. The relationship's ultimate success will be determined by the synergy between the parties—their enthusiasm for the project, shared expectations, a clear understanding of common goals, and frequent and open communication. This will require working hard at getting to know one another's particular core competencies and processes and compromising during the various stages of the production process. To keep this process healthy and transparent, you cannot lose sight of the initial vision that made the idea of exchanging intellectual property a means by which both parties could combine their efforts to provide better products—and more customer value—together than they could alone.

"What's most important is that we get on well with our partners and build a good relationship. Then ideally, they should make prompt decisions, supply their text and approve their proofs efficiently, and pay their bills on time. If they reprint, we love them even more!"

--Catherine Bruzzone Publisher, b small publishing, U.K.

Process Protocol

There is no specific template that will guarantee an effective and efficient process. It will depend on the type of product, the market, and the people implementing the project; how many different steps in the process are necessary; and how complex those steps need to be to accomplish the goal.

However, there are some basic protocols that you should establish that could serve as a road map for ensuring that milestones are met and that each step of the process is validated. Ideally, of course, it's best to prepare a road map of all known and critical issues prior to finalizing a contract.

- ✧ Describe exactly what the licensed content consists of in terms of text, images, and other media assets, i.e., the physical specifications—pages, number of assets, length of each asset, megabytes, etc.

- ✧ Make sure that samples of the original content, either in print or digital format, are available and accessible for every licensed asset.

- ✧ Determine what specifically needs to be adapted or translated.

- ✧ Determine what file formats the licensed assets need to be in and arrange a timetable for having them converted, if necessary, and deadlines for receiving them.

- ✧ Identify what skills and talents will be necessary to carry out the adaptation.

- ✧ Appoint the primary contact people and define their main responsibilities.

- ✧ Determine who should be contacted if there is a problem with a file, if something is missing or corrupted, or if something needs to be changed.

- ✧ Identify who needs to approve the deliverables, who determines whether a file or deliverable is not acceptable, and who on the other side is responsible for making any necessary corrections. Identify the primary stakeholders in the development process and what their roles and responsibilities are.

✧ Decide how you are going to handle any unexpected problems and what the escalation process is so there is always someone available to respond to a problem.

✧ Determine the frequency of progress reviews and meetings—either in person or via phone or videophone (such as SightSpeed, my personal choice, or Skype)—and who is in charge of setting up the meetings and conference calls.

✧ Decide what progress reports you will provide and how they will be made available. Spreadsheets or other types of reports should be made available on an FTP site with folders clearly identified for use by specific members of the development team.

✧ Identify any third parties involved and whether permissions of any kind will be required.

✧ Determine what credits, trademarks, patents, and any other notices will need to be indicated.

✧ Determine who is responsible for applying for local copyrights and any other ownership duties.

✧ Schedule the launch date for the product and make sure that the production process allows for timely completion.

✧ Plan appropriately if multiple formats need to be produced and if there is a compelling marketing reason for sequencing the release of these formats.

✧ Identify other partners who may need to be involved and who should receive the finished product.

Good Processes Make Good Relationships

The goal and measure of a successful relationship is delivering on the plan. In order to execute the plan effectively you need to identify what you are going to provide—or what you expect to receive—and in what format. It is not uncommon, in the early stages of a licensing deal, for the two parties to come to different conclusions about the exchange of content, where false assumptions are made about the nature of the intellectual property, its comprehensiveness, what is included and what is not, or the format that it's in. It's easy to get carried away with the idea of the deal and neglect the importance of being absolutely clear about what you own, what you can license, and what, precisely, you are agreeing to.

You and your partner will save a lot of time and unnecessary misunderstandings if you have a written document that describes the various stages of the content exchange and development process and who on both sides will be authorized to approve the various stages of the process. This document should identify specific benchmarks, what you want to see or check during the process, and a strict schedule for accomplishing the tasks. And, finally, you have to agree on exactly what has to be accomplished in order to determine that both parties have fulfilled their obligations to one another. You can compare it to a "punch list" for completing a construction project. Of course, you can put as much of this in the contract as you can anticipate prior to getting started. But the list will grow as the project advances and changes shape, which means that the contract, as I discussed in the previous chapter, may not be able to account for everything. A good relationship will recognize this.

One of your biggest considerations if you are the content provider is to determine how much freedom you will give your partner in adapting your content. Some content providers have very strict rules for what can or cannot be changed, edited, or expanded upon. At the same time, if these rules are too restrictive, the deal could collapse or you could prevent your partner from making the right marketing decisions.

However, if you are part of a large organization, which may have several different business units responsible for licensing of one kind or another, certain restrictions, such as how the brand is used or how proprietary characters can be depicted, may be dictated as part of a corporate mandate. There may not be a lot of flexibility here. But if you have a lot of control over what you can allow your partners to do, you will find it to your benefit to allow them to adapt the product as freely as possible to meet market needs.

In some cases, there may be covenants surrounding the origination of the content, and this will help to determine how much latitude you can permit. For example, there may be multiple authors or third parties involved, in which case there might have to be several approval stages. Or there might be some very specific cultural content that would not be appropriate for the licensee's market that the licensee might not be aware of. If this is the case, it is essential that you alert your partner to things of this nature in advance.

Naturally, it is desirable to have as much freedom as possible when adapting something for your market, and similarly, a licensee will want maximum flexibility in making any necessary changes and adaptations. Without setting up a baby-sitting process, you and your partner need to build into the process the essential checks and balances that protect the property and the rights of all the copyright holders. At the same time, the process must also allow for the accurate adaptation of the content from one culture to another while making sure that the end result is appropriate for its new market—and that it gets to market without unnecessary delays.

The same flexibility that is built into the development process must also be applied once the product goes to market. Here, too, unexpected issues will arise and you may need to make some adjustments, regardless of what is in the contract, to save the relationship and the profitability of the product.

The following "Case in Point" demonstrates how this can actually work.

A Case in Point

Over the years we had developed a successful multilevel mathematics program that was one of only a few programs in the marketplace that taught math through real-life contexts. The program was the result of a unique collaboration between U.S. and Dutch mathematics scholars who had received a National Science Foundation grant to create a program that made the connection between mathematical concepts and everyday life. Because of its pedigree, the program received notoriety in the international mathematics community, which helped us in our licensing efforts. One of our first licensees was the top Korean mathematics publisher, which was quite a coup since Korea was already a global leader in teaching mathematics.

The publisher did an excellent job of translating and adapting the program so that it conformed to the way in which math is taught in Korea. The program was well received by their sales force, which forecasted ambitious sales numbers.

In Korea, before schools will decide on purchasing one program over another, they test the competitive products thoroughly in hundreds of classrooms—requiring publishers to provide a large quantity of samples free of charge. During the sampling process, an executive at our Korean publisher noticed that our licensing agreement had a free sampling cap of 10% of the print run, which meant that they would have to pay royalties on any free products that they distributed in excess of 10% of the manufactured quantity. No one on either side had paid much attention to this restriction during the negotiation process. If the publisher were to be constrained in this way, however, they would feel compelled to limit their sampling initiative; it would be an onerous burden to pay royalties on free samples while bearing the costs of manufacturing, marketing, and distribution. Having to do so would put them at a disadvantage to a local competitor who was in a position to sample more liberally.

No one makes money by giving product away, so it's important to understand why the 10% ceiling on sampling may have been in the contract in the first place. In theory, a sampling restriction would make sense in preventing someone from giving one product away in order to sell another one. If you are a licensor, you don't want your product used as a premium to sell another product if the only way you can get paid is by earned royalties from revenue. If your product is being heavily sampled, you are at risk of not earning very much.

But in this case, we had a three-year agreement with a substantial minimum annual guarantee, regardless of the earned royalties. This meant that we had protection against abusive sampling. At the same time, with minimum revenue hurdles in place the publisher had no incentive to give away more products than was absolutely necessary to gain market share.

Therefore, there was no reason to enforce a ceiling on sampling. We had mutual interests, and the only way that we could both win was to gain as much market share as possible. If the publisher felt that they needed to sample freely in order to maximize their future sales, they should have the flexibility to do so.

It was an easy decision to make an adjustment in the contract and give them complete discretion with sampling without having to pay royalties so that they could compete in the market without a handicap. If we hadn't given them the freedom to do so, we would have put the long-term viability of the product at risk.

In the end, we told the publisher to treat the program as if they owned it and, as long as they met their minimum guarantees, to do what was necessary to meet the expectations of the market. This paid off. The program was so successful that our royalties exceeded the minimum guarantees and the program became the market leader within 18 months of launch. At the end of the initial term of the agreement, we entered into a long-term commitment with our Korean partner. The sampling program ended up being a small investment in developing a valuable equity for both of us.

Wrapping Things Up

In establishing a good working relationship with your partner, one that transcends the contract and allows both parties to work efficiently, there is probably nothing more important than clarifying who is responsible for what and, above all, who will pay for mistakes, corrections, or things that may not have been anticipated. And you can be sure that this will arise. The licensee may complain that files were not sent in the right format and that they have to convert them, which will result in extra costs, or that they had to hire additional writers to fill content holes that were not expected. There are many ways in which both sides can get into a situation where they are complaining about unnecessary incremental costs. Therefore, it's incumbent on both parties to establish early in the process—prior to the signing of the contract, if possible—who will pay for what. This applies to items that are identified in the deliverables list as well as changes or mistakes that are made along the way.

It's impossible to overemphasize the importance of defining what is or is not an acceptable deliverable. It is at the heart of a smooth partnership and a key element in avoiding the uncomfortable situation of blaming one another for something that went wrong and having to cover for the other person's missteps, which are usually unintentional. Things will go wrong, mistakes will be made, and people will change their minds. That's the nature of any project, and a licensing project is no different. Expect this to happen, plan for it, decide how you will handle "surprises," determine the areas of responsibilities as clearly and fairly as possible, and accept responsibility for whatever share of the project you agree to take on.

Try This!

Create a formal document that spells out the development process for a typical project that can serve as a template or model for others. Since there is no single process that will suit all situations, it will have to be adapted depending on the specifications and requirements of every new project.

Chapter 9

Preventing Buyer's Remorse

As I outlined in the previous chapters, the process of making a deal is fairly straightforward and consists of basic steps that everyone should follow, regardless of the publishing segment or target market. I have attempted to describe these steps generally enough so that they can apply to as many situations as possible, placing particular emphasis on building strong publishing relationships, which should be everyone's starting point. With this well established, you can either build your own list by licensing content and products for your markets or generate incremental revenue by licensing your intellectual property into other languages and markets. These are the primary goals of successful co-publishing relationships, and I hope that I have provided a clear blueprint for achieving them.

"The big profitable languages are German and Spanish because they have both volume and reasonable margins. The smaller European language business has to be very carefully controlled in terms of sales costs because the deals are smaller now and there are many well-brought-up young people who spend a lot of time selling foreign rights that cost more in time than the margin generated. Scandinavian margins are still relatively good. Much of the present and future must lie in China and finding the best path to publishing partnerships. India will also generate volume, but mainly in English."

--Ian Grant
Managing Director,
Britannica, U.K.

Probably the hardest thing to do once you have decided to license or co-publish new products for your market is to determine what products you actually want and then make a decision to acquire them. The mechanics of publishing are easy in comparison to pulling the trigger, even after doing your homework. Let's assume you know your market and competition as well as you need to; you understand the economics of publishing and your internal financial hurdles; and you are prepared to take some measured risks. But all of this can, and often does, lead to a certain amount of inertia unless the right conditions are in place to support international co-publishing projects.

In order to build momentum for co-publishing projects in any publishing company, there has to be an internal environment that supports and values this activity as well as individuals who know how to work within this environment effectively. In smaller publishing companies this is often accomplished by a strong founder or CEO who is personally committed to this kind of business development. But with or without this top-down energy behind international projects, there needs to be individuals with the knowledge, experience, and skills to make good decisions and, equally important, the ability to get inter-company buy-in so that outside projects are enthusiastically received, developed, and marketed as aggressively as internally produced, proprietary products.

I have known experienced publishers and rights managers who understand all of the elements that go into making successful publications but ultimately can't decide what they want to publish or even what they themselves like.

The "Case in Point" that follows is a scenario that I've seen played out many times and at different companies. Sometimes you can find this situation more frequently in larger companies, where there isn't the advantage of a strong personality driving international projects.

A Case in Point

An editor who is responsible and accountable for spearheading acquisitions and buying rights for his company goes to a book fair and discovers an Italian publication that he likes and that he believes will fit in perfectly with and add value to his company's current list of publications. After studying the product carefully, he determines that, other than the translation into English, it will require only a modest amount of work to adapt to one of his key market channels.

He begins to negotiate for the publishing rights, making sure that he covers all of the bases. He asks for worldwide English-language rights, and the publisher agrees. He makes sure that the publisher has cleared all of the photo rights and that there are no restrictions on the maps and other illustrations. The publisher agrees to a fair royalty rate with no minimum guarantees for the initial term of the agreement, which they define as 18 months from the publication date of the English-language edition. The publisher also accepts a modest advance against royalties that will cover the translation work with no additional charges and agrees to make any necessary editorial changes after the translation has been checked for accuracy.

To make the overall co-publishing deal even more attractive, the Italian publisher also has an arrangement with a printer in China that can manufacture the books at an extremely favorable per-unit cost if the editor agrees to have his edition printed at the same time as the French and German editions. The editor agrees and ends up with a deal he thinks will provide an excellent new publication with the potential of returning very good margins on his investment, with only a modest capital expenditure in a short initial print run. So far, so good.

The editor gets back to his office, sends the publisher an NDA to counter-sign, clarifies a few minor points with an exchange of e-mails, and, a few days later, he receives a term sheet covering the points that they had discussed at the book fair. After they confirm that the term sheet is accurate, the publisher sends the editor a first draft of the contract to review. It appears to represent accurately what they had agreed to. Everything seems to be in place.

Then the editor hesitates. He has doubts. He worries that he didn't make the right choice and that he was too hasty in focusing on the Italian publication. He wonders if there isn't something better out there, on the same subject, from another publisher. He asks the publisher to give him more time to think it over. The momentum and enthusiasm for the project begin to wane. Finally, he decides not to proceed and cancels the deal.

To some degree this is natural. We are human, and we often have doubts about making buying decisions, whether it's a house, a car, a new pair of shoes, or a license to publish a book. Some of us who don't like to trust our gut (and don't have the right processes in place to confirm our instincts), have a harder time making decisions than others. We don't want to make the wrong decision, so we make no decision at all.

I've even seen some cases where a rights manager will pay a non-returnable advance—a holding fee—just to review a product on an exclusive basis for a certain period of time and finally decide not to proceed. In some cases, especially if the product will require a substantial investment, paying a holding fee could be a prudent business practice. Better to spend a little up front to review a product carefully—to assess whether it's right for the market and your sales channels—than to later regret making a major commitment of time and money.

However, publishing is more of an art than a science, and you can never know for sure whether a product is going to be a success. There will always be some guesswork at play and some risk. Numerous publishers rejected even some of the most popular current best sellers before someone took a chance on them. This was true for the authors of *Chicken Soup for the Soul* and for J.K. Rowlings when she was trying to find a home for *Harry Potter*. They received many rejections before someone took a risk on these titles—Health Communications Inc. with *Chicken Soup* and Bloomsbury (U.K.) and Scholastic (U.S.) with *Harry Potter*.

Publishing requires good instincts backed up by as much experience and data as possible. If you don't feel that you have developed the instincts necessary to know a good product when you see it, you won't get much out of shopping around at a book fair.

However, good instincts are not enough; even though your instincts can be a valuable tool, you shouldn't have to rely on them exclusively. You should also have a variety of confirming checkpoints and viewpoints within your company that can help you validate your sense of what will or will not work. Malcolm Gladwell in his book *Blink* places a lot of value on expert gut feeling. An experienced publisher's initial reaction **is** often going to be the right one. But when you are working within a corporate structure and you need other people to get behind a project, it's a good insurance policy to get initial reactions verified. Generally speaking, good data should support an experienced publisher's gut feeling.

Rallying the Troops

In the final analysis, it's a question of balance—good instincts vs. validation—and making sure that you have the right process in place before you spend a lot of time asking for concessions from your future partner. Before you begin the negotiations, get as much internal buy-in as possible on a product that you like so that you are confident that the product is right for the market that you are targeting. Have all of the final product specifications available and bring samples back to the office. Show them to as many of the key decision-makers as possible, including your sales managers as well as your distributors. If necessary, assemble a focus group or two, and make sure that you include potential buyers for the various markets that the product can address. Articulate the features and benefits that will make others excited about the product—and that made you passionate about it in the first place.

Your editors and marketers need to believe that the adaptation can be accomplished with minimal resources and effort and that it has the potential to achieve excellent results. Again, it's important to remember that licensing is all about saving time and money. There are opportunity costs that licensing a project are supposed to save. If a project requires too much work and too many resources, you might as well start from scratch.

At the same time, make sure that your finance people believe in the project. For them, it's a question of cash flow, margins, and profitability. In other words, the licensed project should have a minimal impact on cash flow with an above-average ROI. If these stars line up, finance won't hesitate to support the project.

Put together a comprehensive marketing plan, and make sure that your marketing, sales, and promotions people know how to position the product against the competition. Be sure to get approximate marketing costs from them that include pre-publication pricing and sampling, if necessary, as well as brochures and other promotional pieces.

Wrapping Things Up

If your editorial, sales, marketing, promotions, and finance people all like a licensing project, you can validate your initial instincts and have all the confidence you need to negotiate in good faith and close the deal when you are comfortable with the terms of the agreement.

You have to be disciplined enough to go through the steps of the buy-in process. Don't think that the answer to making the right deal is in the negotiation itself. First you have to determine that everyone who needs to will take some ownership of the project. If this happens, you have increased the chances that the licensed product will be successful.

Try This!

Develop a communication process within the company that gets buy-in from everyone who will be responsible for the success of a licensing project. Make sure that editorial, marketing, sales, legal, and finance all agree that the project meets corporate objectives. Every department should own a piece of the project.

Chapter 10

Taking "Yes" for an Answer

Ⅰf knowing when to buy the rights to a particular product or intellectual property is perhaps the hardest thing to learn to do in publishing, the next hardest thing to do is deciding how, when, to whom, and under what conditions you should sell the rights to your IP—your "baby"—either in part or whole.

When you are in the process of acquiring a product, you have to defend against buyer's remorse. As I discussed in the last chapter, to address this problem you should create an atmosphere in your company that makes co-publishing projects a strategic part of your development process. With the right processes in place, there should be no aversion to licensing a project from the outside—and no greater risk in adding a licensed product to your list than in building one from the ground up. In fact, when you consider the smaller number of resources required in licensing and adapting a project as opposed to building one with internal resources, a co-publishing or licensing project should represent a faster way to get to market with less capital expenditure, resulting in a better ROI.

On the other hand, when you are selling rights, you have to learn how to let go of a proprietary asset and allow someone else to take control over its fate in another market. After all, your product or database is a piece of you; it represents a risk that you took, a serious investment of time and resources, and sweat equity. In addition, it represents your brand and reputation. Presumably, it is also bringing in revenues from its primary market. Even in the case of a limited license in a clearly defined territory for a limited period of time, it's not particularly easy to say yes to a co-publishing partner and let someone else take over the responsibility for generating revenues and building the product's value.

What has to be kept in mind is that once you have created a product, your goal should be to reach as many markets as possible with the least amount of risk and the greatest ROI. It's important to maximize the markets you can reach on your own—presumably with the best margins possible—and, at the same time, to identify those markets in which you will need to partner. By licensing a product to someone else you will be decreasing your margin and giving up control, but you will also be penetrating markets that would be otherwise unattainable.

Of course, you should pick your partners very carefully. But once you have done your due diligence and validated a partner's reputation and ability to penetrate a market or channel, licensing your product should be a proactive business development activity. In fact, it should be a strategic activity. Licensing should have the highest corporate priority—with full upper-management support—for building brand loyalty and adding new revenue streams.

If there isn't a corporate culture within your company dedicated to licensing, there could be a lot of unnecessary second-guessing. I've seen this happen at all levels of management when licensing opportunities are presented and they aren't aligned with fully adopted corporate goals. People begin to question the deal as soon as it hits the radar, and objections are raised by those who think that by licensing the product, or a portion of the product, they might lose sales opportunities in their existing channels. They raise a variety of concerns that they believe might interfere with current marketing efforts, which causes unnecessary delays in making the deal and can ultimately lead to the deal's demise.

This is an unfortunate situation to have in any company, large or small. There is a huge global market out there, and most products do not begin to take advantage of it. As a result, in most cases, objections to extending a product's presence in a new market or channel by licensing the rights to a third party are usually invalid. Still, if there are even perceived conflicts, they have to be taken seriously so that licensing can become a growth opportunity that is embraced by the entire management team.

Dealing with Real and Perceived Conflicts

Here are ten common objections that often surface when a deal is up for review.

1. The licensee does not have a large enough market share in his own markets.

2. The royalty rate isn't high enough.

3. The advance isn't large enough to risk channel conflict.

4. The deal might have a negative impact on our brand.

5. The deal will confuse existing customers.

6. The deal will cannibalize internal sales efforts and take commissions away from the sales teams.

7. The licensee's pricing structure cannot be controlled and will lower the value of the product in existing markets.

8. The territory is not restricted enough and will inhibit other licensing deals.

9. The term of the agreement is too long without enough of an upside.

10. The minimum guarantees are inadequate in demonstrating the licensee's confidence in the product.

These are all legitimate concerns, and they need to be fully addressed and answered so that the deal—and future ones—can proceed according to a strategic plan that, through targeted licensing deals, will permit you to take advantage of every opportunity to monetize existing products and provide valuable incremental revenue. In terms of these specific objections and others that may arise, those tasked with selling rights need to be prepared to respond to them and justify the specific terms of the agreement so that the final document is as good as it can be.

It is important to establish parameters that allow the rights people enough flexibility to deal with a wide variety of situations but are also specific enough to cover corporate interests. At the same time, these rules of engagement have to be made available and communicated so that everyone who needs to know is aware of them. Here is a possible set of guidelines, with the caveat that the specifics are meant to be placeholders only.

✓ The licensee has a proven track record and is a market leader.

✓ All IP rights have been cleared for the territory.

✓ There are no conflicting agreements in the target markets.

✓ The licensee will commit adequate resources to complete the project to an acceptable quality standard.

✓ The licensee has a business plan that will meet corporate objectives.

✓ Advances and minimum guarantees will provide an ROI that is commensurate with the size of the market.

✓ The royalty rate is at least seven percent of net receipts.

✓ The initial term limit does not exceed three years.

These guidelines should form a checklist of do's and don'ts, which should be adopted as "standard guidelines for licensing intellectual property" and then represented in a kind of decision tree that is designed to reject bad deals or accept good deals in a timely manner. An effective decision tree will stop a deal before you've unnecessarily encouraged your partner, negotiated with him in good faith, and made a deal in principle. This will serve as an empirical aid to validate your own judgment about the value of the licensing project and the role it plays in meeting corporate objectives.

Any licensing deals that are finalized need to be communicated immediately to the sales and marketing teams so that

"It's time to re-tool. Start totally re-inventing the way we create, manage, and sell our stuff. Re-think the experience, re-think the process and information flow, and remember to optimize, optimize, optimize."

--*Sol Rosenberg*
VP Marketing, Value Chain International, Ltd.

they are fully apprised of new markets that are being served and so they are not surprised if their existing customers become aware of them. The selling teams need to understand that the world is a very large market and that it's impossible to penetrate the number and variety of global opportunities without partners. This means that, whenever possible, various products will be licensed for translation. Most sales teams won't object to this, since it's unlikely that the translated product will conflict with their marketing efforts. But it also means that some products or portions of products, particularly from large databases, may also be licensed to third parties and niche markets in your own language. These efforts may appear to cut into the company's main sales channels. However, there is no reason, in a global marketplace with a vast array of needs to serve, that licensing should interfere with other sales and marketing efforts. Good communication and a strategic plan for making licensing deals that everyone understands and buys into will help to minimize objections and greatly reduce the perception of channel conflict, even among the most protectionist sales managers.

Wrapping Things Up

An important aspect of licensing is the issue of exclusivity. Most licensees will ask for it even if it's not essential in achieving their goals. The theory is that the less competition there is, the easier it will be to differentiate the product, control pricing and discounts, and take advantage of as many channel opportunities as possible. At the same time, people understand that exclusivity comes at a higher price. The buyer would have to pay a lot more to guarantee that no other version of the product has market presence.

In some cases it may make sense to grant exclusivity. If you carefully define languages and/or territories and you get a large enough financial commitment, there may be an advantage in granting exclusivity. However, if you were licensing your content to someone who is limited to a certain technology, such as the Palm operating system, or is only able to reach one market, such as the school or library market, then granting exclusivity beyond a carefully defined market would be a mistake. It gives your partner more freedom than can possibly be exploited and limits your ability to leverage your IP in as many channels as possible. Non-exclusivity will result in smaller guarantees and minimums, but at least you are free to take advantage of other opportunities.

Still, although it may be easier for the IP owner to agree to a deal that is non-exclusive, it may not always be the right decision. In some situations, the price of the freedom to license the property—or even a version of it—to someone else may be costlier than you think. You may be passing up an even larger opportunity with someone who is able to exploit all the markets in a territory, but only through exclusivity.

It all boils down to understanding the market as well as possible and finding the right partner. Maybe it's only one partner under an exclusive arrangement. Maybe it's multiple partners, each with a clearly defined sales channel. In any case, exclusivity should not be granted lightly and should be valued accordingly. It's another tool—perhaps the most important one—that the licensor has to help make the right deal for the right reasons.

Your goal is to take advantage of as many opportunities as possible to monetize your initial investment in a product, and licensing can present some of your best opportunities. Be sure that the guidelines for getting to "yes" are as unequivocal as possible. Once you have guidelines that satisfy that goal, make sure that you empower the right people with as much latitude as possible to exploit those guidelines with minimal interference and second-guessing.

Try This!

You have built content in order to have it work in the marketplace. Try to find as many markets as possible for the end product, even if it means that you will have to give up some control to a partner. There are probably more permutations possible than you may think. Empower someone to go out and look for as many opportunities as possible.

Chapter 11

Publishing's Sea Change

Over the last few years opportunities to benefit from international markets have continued to grow, and the number of countries that can be considered to be viable markets, both as a place to sell products and as a source of new products or services, has also grown. As a result, even more emphasis needs to be placed on how to internationalize products, how to get to as many markets as possible, and how to take advantage of the efficiencies and cost benefits of working with overseas suppliers.

"All our printing is done by one printer in HK/China. We have built up a very close relationship with them and they take on the role of a production department, saving us at least one staff member. As well as providing high quality color printing, they are export specialists, so they can deliver books around the world smoothly and efficiently. Their prices are good but the most important thing is their excellent service."

--Catherine Bruzzone Publisher, b small publishing, U.K.

Seeking less expensive ways to manufacture books, publishers have been printing overseas for decades, first in Hong Kong, then in Singapore and China, and, increasingly, in South America and Eastern Europe. Although this is not new news, the amount and variety of printing that is moving overseas continues to increase. Overseas printers have invested heavily in pre-press and printing technology in order to be able to handle any kind of printing requirement. Consequently, printing and manufacturing overseas is one of the surest ways for publishers to save real money and increase their margins—while maintaining quality and, in most cases, improving the level of service they receive.

Printing is an obvious commodity to outsource because there are many suppliers for most printing tasks from whom you can expect consistently high-quality output. As long as printers remain under enormous pressure to keep their physical assets in constant use and compete aggressively for every job available, publishers can take advantage of the excess supply of acceptable and even excellent printing options. Because this kind of competitive environment is likely to continue in the future, especially as certain kinds of printed products are dropped in favor of electronic publications, there will be many opportunities to lower printing costs on any given job—especially from overseas suppliers. So intense is the competition that the largest global printers based in North America have purchased printers in South America, Eastern Europe, and Asia and can now move jobs to these plants, if necessary, in order to retain high-volume printing contracts.

In spite of the competitive nature of the industry, printing still represents the most expensive part of the publishing process, mostly because of the cost of paper, which continues to rise over time. And even though there are economies of scale as you increase your print runs—the more you print the lower your unit cost—printing still represents a large fixed cost in your P&L. Therefore, as long as you are publishing in print, you need to take advantage of the cost savings that can be achieved from overseas printers.

Beyond Printing

In an electronic format, content can be produced, put on the Web, or made available in a downloadable file for no additional printing or distribution costs. That's one economic advantage that electronic publishing has over print publishing. As a result, publishers need to build their electronic publishing programs while maximizing their print distribution. In most cases, publishers are able to earn the same revenue from an electronic publication as they can from a print product, without all of the added costs of paper, printing, binding, and warehousing.

Still, the overall costs of each stage of the publishing process continue to rise, from the development of good content—especially when illustrated in four-color—to its presentation, storage, and distribution in multiple electronic formats, which require various text and image tagging. In short, electronic publishing comes with its own set of costs and is not, as may sometimes mistakenly be thought, a simple by-product of a print publication.

Because many publishers of electronic products are still experimenting with business models, including making

"Traditional paper is very important but many clients have a Web interest."

--Ben Hill
Managing Director,
Lovell Johns, U.K.

electronic content available free on their Web sites in order to attract advertisers, publishers often find themselves in the position of having to rely on the revenue from their print products to finance their electronic publishing activity. This is particularly true of textbook publishers who have to give away multiple interactive products in order to justify the high price of a textbook, which can easily exceed U.S. $80 even for a standard middle-school textbook. Therefore, as important as it is to find more creative and efficient ways of distributing content on the Web or on mobile devices, it is even more important to turn to certain overseas sources as a means of lowering the costs of generating, manipulating, and formatting content.

In addition to high-end printing, overseas suppliers now offer a variety of services at all levels of the value chain—from format conversion and digitization to content generation and editorial services. This is mainly the result of many years of investment in human resources through education and the sophisticated development of best practices. Whether it's your entire business or part of your business, there are efficiencies to gain in outsourcing certain steps of the electronic publishing process to overseas suppliers.

The Age of Outsourcing

What's happened over the last five years or so is the growth, or rather explosion, of companies, particularly in India, that can provide high-quality services—at lower costs—with little startup time and in response to almost any need. These services, which are known as BPOs, or business practice outsourcing, started out as call centers and primarily provided customer support. Today, BPOs that cater to the publishing industry provide comprehensive and highly scalable publishing services from keyboarding, scanning, and file conversion; to illustration and page layout; to proofreading, indexing, and copyediting; to Web development and software engineering. They are creating new publishing paradigms that are changing the way that we are developing and distributing content.

The growth of BPOs seems almost limitless. If you go to India, or talk to India-based companies, you will also learn about CPOs for content development, PPOs for pre-press and printing services, and KPOs (knowledge process outsourcing) offering legal or accounting resources. India has a large, educated, highly motivated English-speaking workforce, so you can be sure that more "POs" will emerge as the needs arise.

So publishers now have a choice. They can build their own systems and invest in services that they will use only for themselves and end up with cost centers and fixed costs, which eat away at their bottom lines. Or they can take advantage of the infrastructures and best practices that outsourcing companies have built from working with many publishers—on a wide variety of content sources—and use these services only when they need them. In this way, publishers don't have to staff up or down as projects come and go. They can rely on outsourcing companies who can scale their resources according to their client needs and move resources from job to job. By working with many companies, outsourcers are able to re-allocate resources much easier than a single publisher can. For publishers, it's becoming less economical and less productive to have in-house proprietary services when, in many cases, better services are available elsewhere at a fraction of the cost.

We live in the age of outsourcing, and those publishers who do not take advantage of it will not be able to compete in either a global or a domestic marketplace.

It's important to keep in mind that outsourcing is not an end but a means. The efficiencies that result from outsourcing

"Two clients worked very successfully with production houses in India in the past year. [The] key was unexpected high quality and timely responses to changes in plan."

--Tom Murphy
President, Professional Publishing Services

allow publishers to focus on the higher end of the value chain. Publishers need to have the necessary resources to invest in innovation and superior content, the things that differentiate them in the marketplace. Outsourcing helps to free up resources necessary for developing high-quality content, adapting that content for as many markets as possible, and building a story around the content—a compelling marketing message—that makes it attractive to as wide an audience as possible.

Publishers and the Internet

The amount of digital content that is easily and inexpensively available has arguably affected publishing more than anything else in our lifetime. Of course, it is impossible to talk about the accessibility of digital content without crediting the Internet. The Internet has not only changed the actual speed with which we exchange information and content, it has altered our expectations of how fast information can be created and shared as well as how much information we have access to. It has also changed how we regard static versus renewable content and the value we place on information, which is, and will continue to be, a central concern of publishers.

If publishers are going to be successful in the digital age, they must learn to adapt to this new environment, where the amount of information is doubling almost daily; where updates are nearly instantaneous; where we are approaching universal access to almost any kind of information; and where business models are in a constant state of flux. Thus, publishers have to remain keenly focused on how they can add value, which may be different from how they established their value proposition in the past. It may not be enough to know how to create and distribute quality content worldwide. It may also be necessary to leverage key relationships in order to acquire and aggregate relevant third-party content on the one hand, and attract and involve an international community on the other. In short, publishers will have to be skillful at organizing, synthesizing, and connecting diverse forms of content that, at its most engaging, evolves from intimate knowledge of the end user.

As I indicated in Chapter One, knowing what information we can trust is a problem that has increased dramatically as a result of the Internet and the proliferation of millions of Web sites. In order to take advantage of as much **reliable** information as possible in real time, there has to be a way of identifying and distinguishing quality sites from worthless ones. It's a problem that publishers—with their experience in developing authoritative, quality content, and a history in building brand loyalty—are uniquely positioned to solve.

The Internet offers huge advantages and benefits to us in doing our work, improving our skills, and learning more about the world and ourselves. Further, there is no area of human knowledge that has not benefited from how the Internet has enabled the flow of information. It's impossible to underestimate the ways in which the Internet has affected the exchange of information; and it's equally impossible to predict how it will change the way we view and access information and knowledge in the future. What we can say for sure is that we will have to get accustomed to a state of continual adaptation.

Just as we can't predict all of the transformations that will evolve from the power of the Internet and the use of digital content, we also can't anticipate anything that is going to cause the Internet to become obsolete. As far as we can foresee, and as far as we can predict these things, the Internet represents publishing's final frontier. It's the space in which we are going to be working in the future and it doesn't appear to have a challenger. If there is something that is the next best thing, no one is aware of it today. This means that digital content is going to be publishing's building blocks for every product and service that we create.

I don't mean to suggest that physical books are going to disappear any time soon. I don't know that they will, and in previous chapters I showed how

"More and more we are involved in a combined media business—magazines, television, computers, direct sales, and clubs. . . . Today 70% of our business is print and 30% electronic; in the future, it will be 50/50."

--Hans-Peter Gutmann
Gutmann+Gutmann,
Germany

printed books (including this one!) remain a perfectly convenient and economical medium. But even printed books could not be made today without digital building blocks, from typesetting and plate-making to the widespread use of print-on-demand technology, which makes the printing of even tens (as opposed to thousands) of books at a time economical for many, if not all, publishing projects.

But beyond developments in technology that have changed the tools of publishing, digital content has enabled a cultural sea change that has transformed what we publish and has redefined who and what a publisher is. This sea change is manifested in several ways. For average consumers who use or create content, digital content and the Internet have brought about two significant events: the convergence of interactive media and the empowerment of the individual to look and appear like a professional publisher. These are far-reaching phenomena that will continue to influence the way we consume information and are bound to have an impact on what we will experience in the future—even if we don't know exactly what form the products or devices will take.

At the same time, at the top of the corporate food chain, digital media is accelerating the continued consolidation in the publishing industry. This trend will continue to reinforce the importance of branded and authenticated content, and the ability to reach as many markets as possible.

The Convergence of Media

It is no longer the case that publishers can work in only one medium and expect to reach all of their markets effectively.

There is too much diversity in the way that we consume information—depending on where we are, what time of day it is, what kind of technology is available to us, and what our preferences are. Still, depending on the information or its intended audience, sometimes one medium is more appropriate than another, and there is no reason to force the simultaneous use of more than one media when it will not improve the communication or enhance the user experience. For example, I'm pretty sure that the best way for me to present the content you are now reading is either through the printed book you are probably holding or as a digital download that presents the information in exactly the same way but is viewable on your computer or as an e-book. An audio book would be another way to adequately present this content. Indeed, the success of audio books—widely available in all formats including podcasts—demonstrates that they fill several important markets, not the least of which is the sight impaired. In any case, I can't imagine a video or musical backdrop enhancing this particular content. But if I thought I could make my case better by building a Web site using video images, moving text, a slide show, and my son's guitar riffs, it would be technically easy for me to do so.

However, for an increasing amount of information that we consume, it is not uncommon to have several media available to us at once. For a typical news item on a Web site, for example, you might read a few columns of text, view photographs with captions, watch a narrated video, listen to a podcast, respond to an interactive poll, follow a link to another Web site with related content, explore a map, and perhaps send an instant message to the editor or author of the item. For common sources of information on the Internet or via cable or satellite TV, media have converged to provide experiences that we take for granted today, but either weren't available or weren't as easily accessible five years ago.

Not only does content on the Web, or content distributed through other broadcast media, typically contain multimedia elements, but there are now examples of multimedia presentations that are being used exclusively to promote single medium products. For example, book videos, which use elements from print, TV, video, and film, are now being used to promote printed books (fiction and non-fiction)—which may or may not ever be adapted into another medium. Book videos often consist of short movies that dramatize scenes or basic themes from a book and are used as promotional pieces, either as advertising or as teaser content on Web sites that feature books and related content, such as reviews or blogs. On average, book videos run from 20 seconds to 10 minutes in length, and sometimes they are no more complex than interviews with the authors describing their plots or characters. You can see examples of videos of books on *The Book Standard* Web site.

Book videos are to books what music videos are to music; they too were not primarily designed as standalone videos with their own intrinsic value but rather as vehicles for promoting a song and the artist. The development of book videos is an extension of the use of one medium to promote another or a kind of multimedia trailer. We can expect to see more of this, particularly since these multimedia experiences are relatively inexpensive to produce and can be created by almost anyone who is willing to put in the time necessary to master easily accessible software that can run on off-the-shelf hardware.

Individual Empowerment

Individuals are using extremely robust layout and custom publishing programs, photo and video editing tools, and music-mixing software to create professional-looking multimedia experiences and Web sites. Moreover, many blogs, which began life as personal electronic journals, are now regarded as legitimate journalism, if not quite professional journalism. (In order to be professional, journalism and published work in general must be fact-checked, edited, copyedited, proofread, designed, and composed by people who are trained and skilled at these tasks—at least that's my unshakable view.) But the day will come when many of these blogs migrate into mainstream media, particularly as we see more blogs being integrated or linked into the Web sites of respected and branded publications.

Enabled by a variety of digital media, easy-to-use software, and the Internet, individuals can appear indistinguishable from publishers. Custom publishing programs combined with custom printing—print on demand—make it possible for individuals to create, print, market, and distribute content and even books with very little development cost and no investment in inventory. Custom publishing along with Web sites and online fulfillment houses as a distribution vehicle have made it easy for individuals to do everything that major publishers can do. Many individuals—independently filling gaps in the market not being addressed by larger publishers and accessible through the Web—can have a visible impact on buying behavior and the economics of publishing.

While individuals armed with the right software can behave like publishers, publishers, on the other hand, are beginning to follow suit and are behaving more like individuals. The result is that many titles that publishers could not afford to publish because of their narrow appeal or low demand can now be developed. If major publishers do not have to make an upfront investment in a minimum print-run in order to publish economically, they can address niche markets in the same way that boutique publishers do; they can create and publish more books and serve a broader market. In this model, publishers do not have to be entirely focused on producing best sellers. If they can increase the number of titles they offer by taking advantage of custom publishing and print-on-demand technology, and thereby serve a wider market, they can afford to sell fewer units of more titles. They can also continue to keep published books with a low demand available if

"In the 'good ole days' the trick was making it. Today, there's lots of stuff out there. The trick is finding the audience. While it may be a 'long tail' world and you can find your niche, you have to remember to go out and do the finding."

--Sol Rosenberg
VP Marketing, Value Chain International, Ltd.

they don't have to maintain a large stock of each title or manage inventory levels. "Out of print" can be a thing of the past.

This is the economics of the so-called long tail, where hundreds of low-demand units together can be as profitable as the publisher's top one or two best sellers. Where in the past, as a general rule, 20% of a publisher's top-selling books accounted for 80% of the profits, by transferring more titles to a print-on-demand model a greater percentage of titles can contribute to the bottom line, putting less pressure on creating blockbusters. None of this would be possible without the transformation in the entire digital value chain, from the creation of content to its distribution.

Industry Consolidation

In spite of the proliferation of small, boutique, and individual publishers, the publishing industry continues to consolidate. Major publishers are getting bigger, and they continue to build their portfolios in many directions. In particular, large- and mid-size publishers are buying smaller or lesser-known publishers who have competence in digital content development and distribution and who have expertise in migrating new and existing content to the Internet. In this way, traditional publishers gain a few things at once.

✧ They acquire content that is either on the Web or is Web-ready.

✧ They acquire technology and core competencies that they don't currently possess.

✧ They acquire a presence in an existing market that is already subscribing to or buying digital content.

✧ They get to new markets faster.

✧ They eliminate, in some cases, potential competition.

Often, by acquiring niche publishers, major publishers leave a vacuum in the market. If they have acquired too many companies too fast, they sometimes find it difficult to optimize all of their activities and neglect the new markets that they were trying to target. As a result, smaller, boutique publishers jump in to fill the gap. By focusing on this small niche market, they end up doing a better job of serving the market than the larger publisher could. Large publishing houses can usually absorb minor missteps, so the appetite for acquisitions that play in new markets and that build additional competencies continues to grow.

Recently there have been many examples of strategic consolidation in the global publishing industry, which is an acknowledgment that digital publishing and distribution require different skills and an entrepreneurial mindset. It is also validation of the belief in the future of digital publishing. What's worth noting is that even though many of the acquisition targets have been U.S. companies, some of the most significant acquisitions are being made by non-U.S.-based conglomerates. With most of the valuable content now being produced or available in digital formats, major global publishers can more easily acquire products and companies from overseas markets. Today, for companies with the available resources, there are no boundaries, either physical or virtual, to prevent them from becoming even larger and more influential global entities.

Here are some examples.

✧ The British conglomerate Reed Elsevier, which bought Harcourt General in 2001 and a variety of online database companies for its LexisNexis division in 2002-05, including Quicklaw, FactLANE, Applied Discovery, Verilaw Technologies, and Rachel Hollingsworth Court Reporting, Inc.

✧ Britain's Pearson, which had already owned Prentice-Hall, Addison-Wesley, Longman, and Scott Foresman, acquired Dorling Kindersley in 2000, a children's illustrated non-fiction publisher, and, more significantly, the $2.4 billion National Computer Systems (NCS), making Pearson the world's largest technology and custom publishing company. Since 2001 Pearson has continued to extend its *Financial Times* franchise by creating Asian and Chinese-language editions as well as acquiring a stake in India's *Business Standard.*

✧ After acquiring Random House in 1998 and merging it with Bantam Doubleday Dell—acquisitions from the 1980s—Germany's Bertelsmann has been strengthening its investments in digital content producers. By 2005 it became the majority stockholder (over 90%) in the RTL media (TV and radio) Group, which includes assets in Germany, the U.K., Belgium, and Russia, and took over Zomba, the world's largest independent music company, strengthening its joint venture with Sony and its BMG music entertainment company. In 2005 Bertelsmann bought Columbia House, North America's largest DVD distributor.

✧ The Canadian enterprise Thomson Corporation, which owns Macmillan Library Reference, Gale, and Westlaw, has been selling off some of its print-based businesses and in 2004 acquired KnowledgeNet, an e-learning provider.

✧ Over the last four years, Discovery Communications has acquired unitedstreaming, Aims Multimedia, and Clearvue/SVE, giving it a near monopoly on streaming educational video.

✧ News Corporation, which owns Harper Collins, made a huge leap into the online community with its acquisition last year of MySpace.

This is only a small sampling of the consolidation in the industry that has taken place over the last five or six years. Although these acquisitions represent only the tip of an iceberg, they point to several important trends:

✧ The obvious importance of the U.S. market as an area of growth for foreign-based media companies;

✧ The innovation and entrepreneurship that is taking place in the U.S. in digital publishing in all fields; and

✧ The leadership being exhibited by global conglomerates to be truly global in their influence and their investments.

Although much of the aggressive acquisition is being led by creative, forward-looking, growth-oriented European companies with a vision for the future of publishing and a willingness to take risks—and a strategic interest in the global market—they are not the only participants.

India-based companies, flush with capital from outsourcing contracts, are now making acquisitions in North America and elsewhere in order to get closer to their customers. By buying small development, pre-press, and QA companies here and in Europe, they can build stronger bridges to their customers and, at the same time, leverage their lower cost structures and larger labor forces back home. In short, the major outsourcing companies are now buying a stake in the markets that already are their best customers. In this way they can better control the quantity and pace of the workflow and cut down on expensive long-distance business development.

Wrapping Things Up

About once or twice a month, or so it seems, I get an e-mail from a company I'm doing business with overseas telling me about an acquisition or major investment that they just made in Canada or the U.S. Mostly these are companies in India, who really do understand where the expense pains are in publishing and how to relieve them. They are particularly good at providing quality-assurance services and digital publishing solutions, including format conversion, composition, copyediting, proofreading, indexing, and page layout and design. They also do excellent illustration work and Flash development. Sometimes it's a company in Eastern Europe, like the Ukraine or Romania, where they have great software developers, or the Czech Republic, where they do some of the best illustration work and video production on the planet. I take it for granted that many of my partners will increasingly be from outside of the U.S. When I have a project to do, I always ask my staff to send the specs or an RFP to one of our overseas partners to find out how they would do it, how much time it would take them, and what it would cost. I'm no longer surprised when I get the most promising responses from our overseas partners.

As I stated earlier in this chapter, the globalization of publishing isn't new, exactly. It's been going as long as I've been in the business. There is no question that the increased globalization in the industry is a direct result of advances in digital technology and the standardization of processes. But when I work with colleagues from places as far apart and as culturally distinct as India, Israel, Romania, and the U.K., I come to the conclusion that there is something else at play. Technology is only a tool, and it would be of no value if we didn't want to build something with it. I think that what's behind it all—the flow of information; the development of a talented, worldwide workforce; the acquisitions; the sharing of content in all media—is the desire to build a more transparent international community, one without cultural barriers, without censorship, and without traditional boundaries.

Try This!

Today you have to think small as well as big. You should create an environment of entrepreneurship within your company—call it "intra-preneurship"—where people are thinking about cost savings by outsourcing, finding partnerships overseas, and re-purposing content for the increasingly digital world. Work only with people who think like this.

International
Book Fairs

Book Fairs by World Region

Africa

Nigeria International Book Fair	Early May
Zimbabwe International Book Fair	Early August
Cape Town Book Fair	Late June

Asia Pacific

New Delhi Book Fair	Late January
Bangkok International Book Fair	Late March
Asia International Book Fair (Singapore)	Early April
Tokyo International Book Fair	Late April
Nepal Education & Book Fair	Early May
World Book Fair (Singapore)	Late May
Seoul International Book Fair	Early June
APA Australian Book Fair	Mid June
Shanghai International Children's Book Exhibition	Mid July
Beijing International Book Fair	Late August/Early September
Shanghai Book Copyright Exchange Salon	Late October

Europe

Salon du Livre: Paris Book Fair	Mid March
Bologna Children's Book Fair	Late March
MPTV/MILIA	April
Bookworld Prague	Late April
Budapest International Book Festival	Late April
Warsaw International Book Fair	Mid May
World Education Market (Portugal)	Late May
Moscow International Book Fair	September
Göteborg International Book Fair	Late September

Europe *(continued)*

Pisa Book Festival	Early October
Frankfurt Book Fair	Early to Mid October
Istanbul International Book Fair	Late October

Latin America

Bienal do Livro de São Paulo	Mid March
Feria Internacional del Libro de Guadalajara	Late November

Middle East

Cairo International Book Fair	Late January
Jerusalem International Book Fair	Late June
Dubai International Book Fair	Mid July

North America

BookExpo America	Late May
BookExpo Canada	Early June

United Kingdom

London Book Fair	March

Appendix B

Useful Web Sites

A URL A-Z for Information on Publishing and Licensing

The Web sites listed below are either mentioned in this book or relate to the chapter topics. All of these sites have useful information on educational and international publishing, licensing, digital publishing, or the Internet. The brief descriptions provided summarize their primary purpose and in some cases have been adapted from the Web sites themselves.

(AIPPI) International Association for the Protection of Intellectual Property

www.aippi.org

The AIPPI (Association Internationale pour la Protection de la Propriété Intellectuelle) is a Swiss-based, worldwide, non-governmental organization for the research and advancement of intellectual property whose members are developers, academics, and owners of intellectual property.

The Association of American Publishers

www.publishers.org

The AAP is the largest organization of American publishers and deals with matters of general interest to its members. It also acts as an advocate for the publishing industry. The organization's main concerns include intellectual property rights, emerging technology, censorship, international publishing rights, funding for education and libraries, as well as other issues of interest to the publishing community. Recently the AAP has taken a tough stance, and has in fact filed suit, against Google for its controversial efforts to digitize the entire collections of various academic libraries including texts that are not in the public domain.

The Association of Educational Publishers

www.edpress.org

Founded in 1895, the Association of Educational Publishers (AEP) is a non-profit organization in the United States devoted to serving and advancing the supplemental educational publishing industry through r search and information, market opportunities, government relations, professional development, and networking events. Its membership represents the many facets of the educational publishing community, including publishers, service providers, nonprofit associations, schools, researchers, and freelance contributors. With the rapid growth of new educational technologies, AEP members are at the forefront of delivering progressive, educational products and services that address individual learning needs and differences.

Berkery, Noyes & Co.

www.berkerynoyes.com

Berkery is an investment bank that specializes in the publishing sector and has strong relationships in the intellectual property community. They have brokered many mergers and acquisitions between large and small publishing companies.

The Bologna Children's Book Fair

www.bookfair.bolognafiere.it

This is the world's leading children's publishing and multimedia products event. Each spring, publishers, authors and illustrators, literary agents, packagers, distributors, printers, booksellers, and librarians come to Bologna to sell and buy copyrights, establish new contacts, strengthen professional relationships, discover new business opportunities, and get a close look at the latest trends in children's books and new media products.

The Bookseller

www.thebookseller.com

Very much like Publishers Weekly, this is a primary source of reliable news events in the book and publishing industry in the U.K.

The Book Standard

www.thebookstandard.com

Launched in 2005, The Book Standard is an online publication that provides news and current information on book sales, licensing and film deals, reviews, analysis, and commentary on the publishing industry as well as book videos. It's a sister publication to the The Bookseller, listed above.

Bowker

www.bowker.com

The world's leading source for book, serial, and publishing data. The Bowker Web site contains comprehensive databases, including booksinprint.com, ulrichsweb.com, and globalbooksinprint.com. Bowker has more than 150 resources in all media, and provides invaluable information for book stores, libraries, wholesalers, distributors, and publishers. Bowker also provides publishers with International Standard Book Numbers (ISBNs).

Frankfurt Book Fair

www.frankfurt-book-fair.com

Held every October at the sprawling Frankfurt Messe, the Frankfurt Book Fair is the largest and most important publishing event of the year. As the world's largest marketplace for trading in publishing rights and licenses, it is the one annual event that every decision maker in the publishing business must attend. Attendees include authors, publishers, booksellers, librarians, art dealers, illustrators, agents, journalists, information brokers, and the general public.

International Digital Publishing Forum

www.idpf.org

This is the international trade and standards organization for the digital publishing industry. Its members consist of academic, trade, and professional publishers; hardware and software companies; digital content retailers; libraries; and educational institutions. Its primary goals are to build and maintain industry standards and to provide members with up-to-date information on digital publishing.

Licensing Executives' Society

www.lesi.org

The LES or LESI is an international organization of 31 national and regional organizations whose goals are to learn about and promote the licensing, managing, and marketing of intellectual properties rights and technology transfer.

Library of Congress

www.loc.gov

The LOC is a rich source of archival information, including documents, photos, videos, and speeches. It also provides a variety of services to publishers, including International Standard Serial Numbers (ISSNs), Cataloging in Publication (CIP) data, and copyright registration.

Literary Market Place

www.literarymarketplace.com

Literary Market Place (LMP) is the most comprehensive directory of American and Canadian book publishing. LMP is a reliable and mostly up-to-date resource of industry data for publishing professionals, authors, agents, industry watchers, or those seeking to gain entry into the world of publishing. The International Literary Market Place (ILMP) provides similar publishing data for more than 180 countries around the world. Both publications are available in print or online.

London Book Fair

www.londonbookfair.co.uk

This site gives you the information about the events surrounding the London Book Fair, which is the premier spring international book fair. It's a popular destination for publishers, distributors, packagers, librarians, and booksellers from all over the world. It's a compact three-day event that is always well attended. For 2007 it returns to central London at Earls Court.

National Aeronautics and Space Administration

www.nasa.gov

The NASA Web site is a unique resource for images related to space and space exploration. Their images generally can be used free of charge. The Web site indicates that NASA imagery, video, and audio material can be used for educational or informational purposes, including photo collections, textbooks, public exhibits, and Internet Web pages.

Online Dictionary for Library and Information Science

http://lu.com/odlis

Part of Libraries Unlimited, the ODLIS is an A-Z dictionary of approximately 4,200 digital publishing terms. It provides useful, simple definitions to basic terminology used in the publishing industry and on the Internet. The entries define terms adequately but sometimes contain dubious references. For this reason, you should use it with caution and double-check any contextual examples against other sources.

The Podcast Directory

www.podcast.net

More than just a directory, this is actually a database of playable podcasts. You can search by topic and keyword or browse the site alphabetically. You can upload podcasts, which then become part of the database.

Publishers Association

www.publishers.org.uk

The Publishers Association is the leading trade organization serving book, journal, and electronic publishers in the U.K. Similar to the AAP in the U.S., it brings publishers together to discuss the main issues facing the industry and to define policies that will advance the industry.

PublishersLunch

www.publisherslunch.com

PublishersLunch is a free daily newsletter, available on the Web, now shared with more than 30,000 publishing professionals. Each report contains stories from the Web and print press of interest to the professional trade book community, along with original reporting and editorials. It is a reliable source for the latest information on publishing deals and royalties. They also offer a paid publication and service, called *Publishers Marketplace*, which provides expanded coverage on the same general topics that are sent out daily.

Publishers Weekly

http://www.publishersweekly.com

Available in print and online, Publishers Weekly (PW) is a good source of news on international book publishing and book selling. It is part of the Reed Elsevier Group.

Reed Exhibitions

www.reedexpo.com

Also part of the Reed Elsevier Group, Reed Exhibitions claims to be the world's leading organizer of trade and consumer events. They are the organizers of BookExpo America and the London Book Fair, among other publishing exhibitions.

The Software & Information Industry Association

www.siia.net

The Software & Information Industry Association (SIIA) is the principal trade association for the software and digital content industry. SIIA provides global services in government relations, business development, corporate education, and intellectual property protection to companies that are leaders in the digital age. They host a variety of technology events throughout the year, including an annual meeting and awards ceremony.

Smithsonian

www.si.edu

If you go to the Archive section of the Smithsonian site under the "Research Smithsonian" heading, you will find a rich source of content, some of which is in the public domain. The site claims that its archives hold an estimated 50,000 cubic feet of paper documents, seven million still photographs, and thousands of films and audio recordings.

United Nations Cartographic Section

www.un.org

Although this is a poorly organized and incomplete site with dated material, it can be useful for identifying regions of the world that might have issues surrounding their official names and contested territories. It has links to other sites that have more detailed information.

Veronis Suhler Stevenson

www.veronissuhler.com

VSS is a private equity and mezzanine capital investment firm serving the media, communications, and information industries in North America and Europe. They also provide in-depth studies on industry trends.

Webopedia

www.webopedia.com

This is an online dictionary of Internet technology and digital publishing terminology. It provides clear and concise definitions, a pronunciation guide, and a reference section of computer facts.

World Intellectual Property Organization

www.wipo.org

WIPO is a global organization whose mission is the advancement and protection of intellectual property rights, trademarks, inventions, and copyrights.

Appendix C

Sample Licensing Agreement

Licensing Agreement

Made this ___ day of _____, 200_

BETWEEN _____

    For themselves, their assigns and successors-in-business

    (Hereinafter called "the Licensor") of the one part

AND _____

For themselves, their assigns and successors-in-business (hereinafter called "the Licensee") of the other part regarding the illustrated Work at present entitled:

    THE _____

    (Hereinafter called "the Work")

WHEREBY _____ is the exclusive owner of all right, title and interest in and to the Work, and all prior editions and copyrights thereof;

WHEREBY _____, plans to print a revision of the Work in accordance with the Revision Plan;

WHEREBY the Licensee desires to acquire from _____ the right to publish and distribute the Work under the terms and conditions set forth in this Agreement and the attached appendices, which are incorporated by reference herein.

1) **LICENSE.** _____, who guarantees to have full power and authority to make this Agreement, grants to the Licensee the exclusive LICENSE to publish, sell and sublicense third-party distributors that are approved in

advance by _____ to sell the **Work in the English language throughout the world in print form only.**

2) **WARRANTY.** _____ warrants that the Work is an original work, that it contains nothing obscene or libellous and is in no way an infringement of existing copyright and that, upon revision, will comply in all material respects with the Revision Plan; that it has full power to make this Agreement and grant the Licensee the rights set forth herein and, in accordance with Clause 23 below, will indemnify the Licensee against any loss, injury or damage occasioned to the Licensee in consequence of any breach of these warranties.

3) **GRANT OF RIGHTS.** The Licensee shall publish, sell and sublicense third parties to sell the said Work as defined in Appendix A in the above-mentioned language throughout the world in print form through all channels. No electronic publication of the Work by the Licensee is permitted under this Agreement.

4) **ASSIGNMENT. SUBLICENSE.** This Agreement and the LICENSE granted hereunder may not be assigned or, except as set forth herein, sublicensed by either party without the prior written consent of the other party, such consent not to be unreasonably withheld. _____ hereby approves the sublicense by Licensee to _____ ("_____") of all rights to distribute the Work granted the Licensee hereunder.

5) **LICENSE TERM.** All rights granted under the terms of this Agreement shall automatically revert to _____ **5 (five) years from the signature of this Agreement**, without any further notice and without prejudice to any monies already paid or then due.

In addition, the rights granted the Licensee in this Agreement are subject to the proviso that if the Licensee places a reprint order of at least 3000 copies the LICENSE period shall be extended by an additional three years from the date of the order, and by a further year for each additional 1000 copies up to a maximum of 5 additional years.

The LICENSE period shall automatically be extended by further periods of one year at a time, if the Licensee keeps the Work in print, unless terminated by either of the parties by written notice at least 3 (three) months before the date of termination.

6) QUANTITY, PRICE & DELIVERY.

_____ Shall produce and sell to the Licensee and the Licensee shall buy from _____ **5,000 (five thousand) complete copies** of the Work, _____ complete copies of which Publisher immediately will distribute to its sublicensee, _____, as indicated in Clause 4 above, at a price of **$00.00 (_____ U.S. dollars) inclusive of royalty, CIF East Coast port** or such other place as the Licensee and _____shall designate in writing at any time and from time to time.

The copies of the Work shall be delivered **on or before** ___ _____, **200_** to the East Coast port.

The copies shall be delivered on or before such date provided that the payments due under **Clause 7 below** have been made by the Licensee and that the material listed in Clause 12 below is received by _____ from the Licensee complete and in good condition by the date stipulated in Clause 12 below, as well as from all other parties participating in the same printing.

_____ shall make every effort to deliver the number of copies specified above, but delivery of up to **5% (five per cent) over or under** the quantity specified shall constitute full delivery. The Licensee shall pay for the quantity of copies actually received. If _____ fails to deliver bound books in good condition **on or before** __ _____ **200_**, the final payment due **60 (sixty) days** after the delivery of full consignment shall not be made until **60 (sixty) days** after the actual delivery date; provided, however,

_____ shall use best efforts to notify the Licensee of any changes to the final delivery date.

The Licensee and all approved sublicensees must complete the attached delivery information as requested in Appendix B.

7) **TERMS OF PAYMENT.**

The Licensee shall pay _____ the following guaranteed non-refundable sum for the quantity of sets specified in **Clause 6 above: $000,000 (_____ US dollars), payable as follows:**

> **$00,000 (____ dollars), payable within three (3) working days of signature of this agreement by both parties;**

> **$00,000 (_____ dollars), payable on completion of all editorial work and revisions (the "Editorial Changes") and approval by the Licensee of the Editorial Changes within the timeframe set forth in Clause 13 below;**

> **$00,000 (_____dollars), payable on receipt of Printer Proofs (as defined below), including covers, by the Licensee and approval by the Licensee of the Printer Proofs within the timeframe set forth in Clause 13 below;**

> **$00,000 (_____dollars), payable upon receipt of notice by the Licensee of the start of printing;**

> **$000,000 (_____ dollars), payable on delivery of finished sets to US East Coast port or such other place as the Licensee and _____ shall designate in writing at any time and from time to time or on __ ____ 200_, whichever is the sooner.**

> **The balance, taking into account any adjustment for the actual**

number of sets delivered, payable 60 days after delivery of finished sets to US East Coast port.

8) **PRICE GUARANTEE. CONDITIONS.** The price for each copy specified in **Clause 6 above** is calculated using prices quoted to _____ _____ by the suppliers on the basis of the following time limits:

Materials costs guaranteed until ___ ____200_
Labor and machining costs guaranteed until ___ ___200_.

The final purchase price shall only be increased from the price specified in **Clause 6 above** if _____'s suppliers have increased their prices by at least 5% (five percent) from __ _____ 200_.

9) **PAYMENTS.** All payments due under the terms of this Agreement shall be made by check in U.S. dollars to _____'s bank account as specified below or as subsequently notified in writing, without provision for returns and without any deduction in respect of taxation, exchange, commissions or otherwise, with the sole exception of tax withheld under bilateral fiscal agreements between _____'s and the Licensee's governments.

Bank:

Account number:

Sort Code:

10) **FULL TITLE.** _____ shall reserve full title in all volumes and materials supplied to the Licensee under the terms of this Agreement until all monies and materials due from the Licensee for such volumes have been received. All materials supplied by _____ are solely for the production of the Work for Licensee: they cannot be used by sublicensees or others without the prior written consent of _____, which shall not unreasonably be withheld. _____ hereby consents to the use of

the materials by ___ in connection with copies of the Work produced for _____ hereunder.

11) **RIGHTS RESERVED.** The copyright in the Work shall remain vested in _____ throughout the term of this Agreement and all rights other than those specifically granted herein are retained and reserved by _____ _____.

12) **COPYRIGHT NOTICES.** The Work shall include on the verso of the title page the following copyright notice:

> ©200_ _____

> Devised and produced by _____

Together with the Licensee's or an approved sublicensee's own copyright notice and other relevant acknowledgments.

Due prominence shall be given on the cover and jacket and in the preliminary pages of the Work to the name of the editor(s).

13) **DEVELOPMENT OF THE WORK; LICENSEE STANDARDS.**

(a) **REPORTING AND APPROVAL PROCEDURES.** Periodically, as requested by Licensee, _____ shall submit to the Licensee a written report providing details of _____'s progress respecting the revision of the Work in accordance with the Revision Plan. Periodically, unless otherwise agreed in writing, _____ shall send to the Licensee printouts or electronic files of the text changes for approval. In the event that the Licensee rejects any Editorial Changes submitted to it by _____, _____ shall modify such changes to the extent necessary to obtain the Licensee's approval. The Licensee recognizes that prompt approval of the Editorial Changes is critical to an efficient editorial process and agrees that its goal will be to respond within five (5) days after confirmed receipt. If the Licensee does not respond within seven (7) days after confirmed receipt, _____ may assume Licensee's approval of the Editorial Changes in question. Any revision required of _____ by the Licensee shall be completed by _____ at its own expense. _____ agrees that no new or additional material shall be included in the Work without the prior written consent of the Licensee, which consent shall be provided or withheld at the Licensee's sole discretion. As soon as possible, _____ shall provide the Licensee with final color proofs of those parts of the Work that require new color images (the **"Printer Proofs"**). The Licensee shall have five (5) days after confirmed receipt to approve the Printer Proofs. If the Licensee does not respond within seven (7) days after confirmed receipt, _____ may assume the Licensee's approval of the Printer Proofs. In the event that the final Work differs materially from the Revision Plan, Editorial Changes or Printer Proofs provided by _____ to the Licensee and approved, either proactively or due to lapse of time, by the Licensee hereunder, the Licensee, in its sole discretion, can demand that _____, at its own expense, modify the Work to the extent necessary to conform from the Revision Plan, Editorial Changes or Printer Proofs, as the case may be.

(b) **LICENSEE STANDARDS.** (i) _____ recognizes that Licensee's reputation as an international publisher is based on the maintenance of high standards in editorial work, manufacturing and in the promotion, distribution and sale of its products (the **"Licensee Standards"**). _____ agrees that similar standards must be maintained in respect to its own production and publication of the Work.

(ii)   The parties agree that the Licensee Standards for editorial material require that the Work be accurate in content, fair and unbiased, up to date and written consistent with the editorial quality of the Licensee's publications. Whether or not the edited material submitted by _____ to the Licensee meets the Licensee Standards shall be a matter for the Licensee to determine. _____ agrees, at its own expense, to revise any material so as to bring it up to Licensee Standards. The Licensee agrees that the prior publication of the Work meets the Licensee Standards.

(iii)   The parties agree that Licensee Standards for manufacturing require that the Work be manufactured, printed and bound with good quality, sturdy materials comparable to premium reference materials currently published in the Territory. The Licensee acknowledges that _____ is well regarded as a quality developer and manufacturer of products similar to those contemplated hereby and agrees that the manufacturing standards generally used by _____ as of the date of this Agreement satisfy the Licensee Standards for manufacturing.

14) DELIVERY BY LICENSEE

(a) **IMPRINT, LOGO, BARCODE, and ISBN.** The Licensee shall supply _____with a CD of its, or its approved sublicensees' imprint details, barcode, ISBN and logo by ____ _____ 200_. Such material shall be for printing in black, to fit _____'s layout.

(b) **COVER.** _____ shall pass to the Licensee sample dummies for preparation of covers. The Licensee shall supply _____ with electronic files plus Printer Proofs of its cover design, or the cover design of any approved sublicensees, by ____ __ 200_.

It is the responsibility of the Licensee to ensure that said electronic files are full and complete and can be passed directly to _____'s printer.

15) ADVANCE COPIES. _____ shall supply the Licensee with 5 (five) advance copies of the Licensee's and each approved sublicensee's editions of the Work prior to the date of delivery of the full consignment of books, two copies from each edition shall be free of charge and inclusive of freight.

Any additional advance copies and their delivery shall be paid for by the Licensee.

16) **COMPLIMENTARY COPIES.** _____ shall retain from the quantity to be delivered **10 (ten)** sets of the Work, these copies shall be paid for by the Licensee. _____shall be permitted to purchase further copies of the Work from the Licensee at manufacturing cost plus cost of delivery.

17) **PUBLICATION.** The Licensee shall publish the Work **within 3 (three) months of delivery.** If the Licensee fails to do so, all rights herein granted shall automatically and without further notice revert to _____ and the advance payments provided for in **Clause 6 above** shall be forfeited without prejudice to any claim which _____ may have for damages, compensation or otherwise.

The Licensee shall give notice to _____ of the dates of first publication, the standard retail prices and all alterations to those published prices within two weeks of their happening.

18) **REPRINTS AND REVISIONS.** The Licensee shall notify _____ _____ in good time when reprints are required and subject to the terms of this contract the Licensee shall have the right to reprint the Work. The parties shall negotiate in good faith the terms including the price for such reprints subject to reasonable minimum quantities being mutually agreed.

19) **REMAINDERS.** The Licensee may not remainder the Work within two years of publication without the written consent of _____. Before remaindering, all copies shall first be offered to _____ at the Licensee's manufacturing cost. _____ shall have 10 (ten) working days from receipt of the Licensee's notification of intent to remainder, in which to confirm that _____ shall purchase part or all of the remaining stock of the Work.

On remaindering the Work, all rights granted under the terms of this Agreement shall automatically revert to _____ without prejudice to any monies due to _____ from the Licensee.

For the purposes of this Agreement the term "Remainder" shall mean the reduction of 75% (seventy-five percent) or more from the price at which the Licensee's edition was first offered for sale.

If the Licensee wishes to remainder only a portion of its stock, he shall obtain _____'s prior written permission, which shall not be unreasonably withheld. Rights shall then automatically revert when the balance of the stock not remaindered is sold.

20) **REVERSION OF RIGHTS.** If the Licensee does not keep an edition of the Work in print and allows it to remain out of print for more than 6 (six) months without coming to an agreement with _____ regarding a reprint, then all rights in the Work herein granted shall immediately revert to _____ without any further notice and without prejudice to any monies already paid or then due.

For the purposes of this Agreement, **out of print is defined as having less than 100 (one hundred) saleable sets in stock** of the Licensee's editions of the Work.

The Licensee shall use its best efforts to inform _____ in writing as soon as the Work goes out of stock, unless it has already placed an order for the immediate reprint of the Work.

21) **ILLUSTRATION RIGHTS.** _____ hereby notifies the Licensee that permission has been granted by the copyright holders to reproduce all illustrations included in the Work (including photographs, artwork, drawings, diagrams and maps) for publication in the above-mentioned territories, but only in the form of the complete page layout supplied to the Licensee _____. This includes permission to reproduce single or double page layouts from the Work for use in catalogues, promotional brochures, as part of a review in a trade or specialist magazine, or as part of a press campaign.

Permission has not been granted for the use of illustrations other than in the form of the complete single or double page layout. On request from the Licensee regarding specific illustrations, _____ shall, where possible, supply the name of the rights holder(s).

Where rights are controlled by _____, specific illustrations may be reproduced by the Licensee for jacket, publicity or other purposes only after having obtained the prior written consent of _____, and on terms to be mutually agreed in writing. Reproduction of artwork shall, when possible, be permitted by _____ free of charge.

For illustration rights that are not controlled by _____, permission and payment for the use of such specific illustrations shall be negotiated directly between the Licensee and the rights holder(s).

In the event of unauthorized use of illustrations of any kind by the Licensee, _____ shall not be liable for any action by the rights holder of such illustrations arising from any such unauthorized use.

"Unauthorized use" means use of illustrations of any kind on promotional literature, advertising or on jackets except in the form of the complete page layout supplied by _____without the written consent of the rights holder and payment of any fees due. "Action by the rights holder" means legal action, increased fees or any other kind of punitive action arising from use of illustrations without the prior written consent of the rights holder and payment of any fees due.

22) **RIGHT OF FIRST REFUSAL.** _____ hereby grants Licensee a right of first refusal to the exclusive license to publish, distribute and sell any single-volume work in print form that is comprised of the entire first set of the Work. _____ agrees to give Licensee written notice of the terms upon which it is prepared to license such rights to a third party, and Licensee shall have forty-five (45) days to deliver its notice of acceptance of such terms. If Licensee fails to accept the offered terms within such forty-five

(45) days, _____ shall be free to enter into an agreement with a third party for the license of such rights, provided that the terms granted such third party shall be no more favorable than those offered to Licensee.

23) **MUTUAL INDEMNIFICATION.** Each party (the **"Indemnifying Party"**) will defend, indemnify, and hold harmless the other party, and its officers, directors, agents, affiliates, and employees, and each of them (the **"Indemnified Party"**), from and against any and all losses injuries, claims, demands, liabilities, costs or expenses, including reasonable attorneys' fees and disbursements (**"Claims"**) to the extent arising out of: (1) the dishonest, fraudulent, negligent, willful or criminal acts of the Indemnifying Party or the Indemnifying Party's employees, agents or representatives acting alone or in collusion with others; and (2) any breach by the Indemnifying Party of any of its representations, warranties, covenants or other obligations under this Agreement. In addition, _____ hereby agrees to indemnify Licensee from and against any and all Claims to the extent arising out of any allegation that the Work infringes the intellectual property rights of any third party. The Indemnified Party agrees that it will (i) provide prompt written notice to the Indemnifying Party of any Claim with respect to which it seeks indemnification and (ii) permit the Indemnifying Party to assume the defense of such Claim with counsel reasonably acceptable to the Indemnified party. If such defense is assumed, the Indemnifying Party will not be subject to any liability for settlement made by the Indemnified Party without the Indemnifying Party's consent (but such consent will not be unreasonably withheld). If the Indemnifying Party elects not to assume the defense of a Claim, the Indemnifying Party will nonetheless be obligated to pay the fees and expenses of the Indemnified Party's counsel. The Indemnified Party reserves the right, at its own expense, to assume the exclusive defense and control of any matter otherwise subject to indemnification by the Indemnifying Party hereunder, and in such event, the Indemnifying Party shall have no further obligation to provide indemnification for such matter hereunder.

24) **CONFIDENTIALITY.** The parties acknowledge that during the term of this Agreement, either of them may receive from the other "Confidential Information" of the other. As used herein "Confidential Information" means information and know-how related directly or indirectly to the disclosing party, its business, or its products that is conspicuously marked "CONFIDENTIAL," "PROPRIETARY," or with other words of similar import, or that the receiving party knows or reasonably should know is not publicly available. The receiving party shall not use or disclose Confidential Information except in connection with, and as contemplated by, this Agreement. The receiving party shall use at least the same degree of care to avoid disclosure or unauthorized use of Confidential Information as it employs with respect to its own most confidential and proprietary information, but at all times shall use at least reasonable care. The receiving party shall not have any obligation of confidentiality with respect to any information that (a) is already known to the receiving party at the time the information is received from the disclosing party, as proven by prior documents or records of the receiving party; (b) is or becomes publicly known through no wrongful act of the receiving party; or (c) is rightfully received by the receiving party from a third party without restriction. Notwithstanding the foregoing, each party is hereby authorized to deliver a copy of any such information (a) to any person pursuant to a subpoena issued by any court or administrative agency, (b) to its accountants, attorneys or other agents on a confidential basis and (c) otherwise as required by applicable law, rule, regulation or legal process including, without limitation, the US Securities Act of 1933, as amended, and the rules and regulations promulgated thereunder, and the US Securities Exchange Act of 1934, as amended, and the rules and regulations promulgated thereunder. The parties shall not make public the terms of this Agreement except by mutual consent.

25) **FORCE MAJEURE.** Anything herein contained to the contrary notwithstanding, neither party shall be liable or deemed to be in breach to the other by reason of any act, delay or omission, caused by epidemic, fire, action of the elements, strikes, lockouts, labor disputes, governmental law, regulations, ordinances or order of a court of competent

jurisdiction or executive decree or order, act of God, or of a public enemy, war, riot, civil commotion, earthquake, flood, accident, explosion, casualty, embargo delay of a common carrier, inability to obtain labor, material, facilities, transportation, power or any other cause beyond the reasonable control of either party hereto, or for any act, delay or omission not due to the negligence or default of either party hereto; provided, however, that if any such cause precludes performance, in whole or in part, by either party for a period of ninety (90) consecutive days, the other party shall have the right to terminate this Agreement by providing written notice to the other party.

26) **FAILURE TO COMPLY.** Should the Licensee at any time himself, or anyone acting on its behalf, fail to submit or comply with the terms of this Agreement in any substantial way, or if the Licensee shall go into liquidation (other than voluntary liquidation for the purpose of reconstruction only) then this Agreement shall thereupon automatically terminate and all rights herein granted shall immediately revert to _____without prejudice to any claims _____ may have for damages or otherwise.

27) **LATE PAYMENTS.** _____ shall notify the Licensee in writing of any overdue payments. _____ reserves the right to charge 1% (one percent) interest for each month or any part thereof on any overdue payments, without prejudice to any other measures _____ may employ to recover any and all monies due.

28) **INFRINGEMENT.** Subject to Clause 23, if at any time during the term of this Agreement any infringement or threatened infringement of copyright affecting the Work shall come to the notice of either party, thereupon such party shall promptly give notice in writing thereof to the other and the parties shall thereupon consult as to the course of action to be followed and each shall render reasonable assistance to the other.

Should notice be served by either party on the other for infringement of any Clause in this Agreement, such notice shall be sent both by fax and by express registered post to the address shown above or subsequently notified and shall be deemed to have been received within five working days from posting.

29) **LIQUIDATION.** Should _____ go into liquidation other than voluntary liquidation for the purposes of amalgamation only, then the Licensee shall have a continuing right to sell the Work for the duration of the Term granted herein. If the Work shall not already have been completed and delivered to the Licensee by the date of any such involuntary liquidation, and if there is no prospect that the Work can subsequently be completed and delivered, then the Licensee shall have the right to offset against sums otherwise payable by it to _____ an amount equal to but not greater than the value of any advances paid by the Licensee to _____ as a contribution to the development cost of the Work.

30) **GOVERNING LAW.** This Agreement shall be deemed to have been made in _____ and any controversy which shall arise out of or relating to the interpretation or execution of this Agreement shall be settled according to the statutes of _____.

Any difference or dispute which may arise between the parties hereto as to the construction, meaning, operation or effect of this Agreement or any Clause or provision thereof or as to the rights, duties or liabilities of the parties hereunder or otherwise in connection with this Agreement shall be referred to a single arbitrator to be agreed between the parties hereto, or, failing agreement, to be appointed by the _____ and in accordance with and subject to the Arbitration Act, 1950 or any statutory modification or re-enactment for the time being in force. The Arbitration shall be held in _____.

31) **HEADINGS.** The Clause headings in this Agreement are solely for ease of reference and shall not affect the interpretation of this Agreement.

32) **VALIDITY.** This Agreement shall be rendered invalid and _____
___ shall be at liberty to license the rights herein granted to a third party
if countersigned copies of this Agreement are not received by _____
within one month of the date of this Agreement.

For and on behalf of
Licensor:

For and on behalf of
Licensee:

_____

_____

Acknowledgments

Writing a book is a solo act, but although you have to please yourself in the end, you are also constantly aware that it's only worth doing if someone else cares as well. Throughout the process of writing this book, I'm thankful to many people who were eager to see it published. In particular, I was motivated by Charlene Gaynor, CEO of the Association of Educational Publishers, my publisher, friend, and advocate. Charlene has done more for the cause of educational publishers than anyone I know, and I'm grateful for her support and for wanting to publish this book. Charlene's director of communications, Stacey Pusey, did an excellent job shepherding the project and getting it into a publishable state.

I want to thank all of my colleagues at Britannica, whose daily hard work and dedication help me remain committed to this wonderful industry. In particular, I need to thank Jorge Cauz, Britannica's president, who has been expertly leading Britannica during a time of tremendous change, as well as my staff, who are the most talented publishing and technology professionals in the business. And especially Ruth Kos, the best executive assistant I have ever had. Their standards are industry benchmarks.

I'd like to express my gratitude to my colleagues in the industry, here and abroad, who were kind enough to take time away from their summer vacation to provide me with invaluable insights from their publishing experiences. They include Sol Rosenberg, Catherine Bruzzone, Tom Murphy, Dave Oliphant, Ian Grant, Ben Hill, Ellen Bialo, Peter Gutmann, and Sebastian Gutmann.

Domo arigato to my great friend and confidant, Danny Asher, who fed me sushi to keep my neurons energized during the process.

Finally, I'm indebted to my wife, Kathleen, and children—Monica, Rachael, and Daniel—who put up with the many nights and weekends when I remained immune to the usual family activity in order to complete this book on schedule.

Index

Printed in the United States
68189LVS00006B/131